Imp
The ImPerfect Pup

LESSONS ON BEING GOOD ENOUGH

By
Jody Rosengarten

Illustrations by Christina Swanke

Design & Production by Patty Volpacchio

To Bell, Peggy, Harry, Lady, Beckett, Algunza, Mowgli, Rosie, Plain Jane (PJ), Monty, Mariah, Déjà vu (DJ), ReRun, Drummer, Buddha, Kiana, Prozac, Stinky, Hodge Podge, Cozy, and Doc, my past and presents dogs. All but Bell and Peggy, my childhood Dachshunds, were rescued. Sharing everyday of my life with these and countless other critters has made me the person I am proud to be.

"We need another and a wiser and perhaps a more mystical concept
of animals. Remote from universal nature and living by complicated
artifice, man in civilization surveys the creature through the glass of his
knowledge and sees thereby a feather magnified and the whole image in
distortion. We patronize them for their incompleteness, for their tragic
fate for having taken form so far below ourselves. And therein do we
err. For the animal shall not be measured by man. In a world older and
more complete than ours, they move finished and complete, gifted with
the extension of the senses we have lost or never attained, living by voices
we shall never hear. They are not brethren, they are not underlings: they
are other nations, caught with ourselves in the net of life and time, fellow
prisoners of the splendour and travail of the earth."

—Henry Beston

The Outermost House: A Year Of Life On The Great Beach Of Cape Cod

Contents

FOREWORD
MY MOWGLI'S STORY

One sweltering July, I dogged a dense-coated stray around the Upper West Side of Manhattan with my rescued German shepherd in tow. On day 10, the stray stepped in front of a city bus as it crept to a halt, grazing him. Though he wasn't seriously hurt, the dog was disoriented enough for me to finally grab hold of him. I called this wolf look-alike Mowgli.

A crowd of dog walkers and others gathered round. After each onlooker protested more vigorously than the last why they couldn't take Mowgli, I agreed to keep him for one week while the others figured out what to do with him.

Being young and stupid, I went out for a bite that first night leaving both dogs in our studio apartment and came home to find Mowgli in the brownstone's lobby. He had chewed through the wall. Despite multiple opportunities to escape according to neighbors, Mowgli waited downstairs for me to return.

With our fate suddenly sealed, I rehabilitated Mowgli by the seat of my pants and found the process so exhilarating that I've devoted every day since to the wellbeing of dogs. That was 1980. Mowgli and I were together for fourteen years.

PREFACE

I had three dogs when I started writing this book a few weeks ago and now I have four—and I didn't even know I was expecting. I adopted seven-week-old Cozy on the day she was scheduled to be killed in a shelter just for being. Cozy is charming, a handful, exasperating and the apple of my eye. Cozy is EveryImp.

Introduction

The world doesn't need another dog training book, but it sure could use *Imp, the ImPerfect Pup: Lessons on Being Good Enough*, a lighthearted look at the serious matter of a person's Perfectionism screwing-up the dog. As a dog trainer behaviorist, with thirty-five years and thousands of dogs under my belt, I witness Perfectionistic overreaching that results in underachieving dogs being abandoned or abused.

It is estimated that only one out of every one hundred dogs born will ever find a permanent home. Of those relinquished, "bad behavior" is identified as the primary problem. I believe unrealistic expectations are the actual culprit.

Today, alone, I received two frantic phone calls from new puppy parents. The first woman was hysterical that her ten-week-old Goldendoodle, "still pees in the house," and the second man complained that, "Pavlov rolled in something putrid." Neither caller was pleased when I said, "That's what dogs do." But that *is* what dogs do.

I have also found that the more power a person wields, the harder the fall. No dewy-eyed, crotch-sniffer's going to undo a CEO, damn it! If Imp poops in the dining room, dismantles an iPhone or refuses to come when called, clearly the beast is defective, justifying harsh intervention or "its" removal.

For some, the pluses of a pristine lawn and noseprint-free windshield outweigh the appeal of a dog. Fair enough—I discourage people from taking one on all of the time. But for those who recognize that the inconvenience is inconsequential relative to the abundance, this book promises results.

Practical goals are paired with no-nonsense training and behavioral tools in a manner that's as entertaining as it is instructive. Vignettes from counseling rich and famous and everyday dog parents, plus tales of my own colorful menagerie, illustrate what's possible without breaking a sweat. Sophisticated behavioral concepts and multi-tiered exercises are personalized to accommodate individual lifestyles and sensibilities. Imp's point of view is always presented.

When I'm in the midst of a glorious meal or book, movie or vacation, looking forward to sharing the wealth with friends is an essential part of my own pleasure. I adore dogs and am sharing my "wealth" here to ensure your relationship is all it can be. I will try (hard) not to romanticize dogs whose love is no more unconditional than anyone else's—it's just that their conditions are more pure.

Whether you buy a shiny new puppy or adopt a weathered elder who's been around the block, this book is designed to make your Good Enough home Imp's last. That said; I will also support the thoughtful person's painful decision to responsibly rehome Imp when absolutely necessary. Even extensive counseling fails to salvage every marriage.

Dogs have broken my heart and one bit me badly just last year. Having made a thirty-five-year career teaching dogs and their people to get along, accepting Imp's shortcomings has taught me to be more fully human.

Imp, the ImPerfect Pup celebrates dogs as they actually are while denouncing the perils of Perfectionism in lieu of its gentler kin, Good Enough. I think Good Enough is a Perfect goal.

CHAPTER 1

Perfectionism's Many Faces

P erfectionism is the voice of the oppressor." Ever since reading these words over a decade ago in Anne Lamott's book, *Bird by Bird*, I've observed that the most miserable people I know are the most Perfectionistic. Whether striving for the Perfect photo, mate, biceps or *soufflé*, Perfectionists drive themselves, and many around them, crazy while pursuing this mythical goal.

Perfectionism takes many forms, and we all seem to have certain leanings. I am rather sloppy about my own appearance but can get positively OCD about arranging my *tchotchkes*. Even as I write, I'm resisting the overwhelming temptation to agonize over each and every single solitary (solitery?) word. Perfectionism has its place, of course. I was thrilled that the neurosurgeon who repaired my brain aneurysm was a card-carrying Perfectionist, and NASA would be $125-million richer if only that measurement hadn't been off by a smidge, but the notion of Perfectionistic puppy rearing is oxymoronic, so why set yourself up to fail? I paid a house call to a couple whose manicured front yard included a poodle topiary but their kitchen had green slime scaling the walls. The husband waxed loftily about the Yorkshire Terrier's pedigree while the wife teased the dog's bangs, yet neither bothered to pick up the poop oxidizing in the corner. The purpose of my visit? To teach Pudding to "sit pretty."

From Broad-Spectrum Perfectionists to Perfection Specialists, different shades of Perfectionism will be addressed throughout the book. But first, if you're still on the fence about getting a dog, please consider the following:

Imp As Equalizer

I have worked with Grammy, Emmy, Golden Globe, Tony, Academy Award winners and a Pulitzer nominee. I've worked with a quadriplegic, shut-ins, a multiple-amputee, paranoid schizophrenics and even some Republicans.

I've seen neighbors whose decade-long Hatfield and McCoy-like feud ended when one fell in love with the other's pup. My curmudgeonly mailman now beams when Cozy races over to say, "Hey!" I have traveled the world and traversed racial, socio-economic and language barriers and I've learned that we are one in Dog's eyes.

How Good Is Enough?

Every morning when my beloved mutt, Déjà Vu (DJ), senses I'm awakening, he tiptoes over to snatch the scrunchy out of my hair and then runs two victory laps around the house before returning to bury it beneath the bed and stroll off all la-di-da. Every morning. Currently, Buddha is sound asleep upside down on the sofa with all four feet in the air and her head's spilling to the floor as she dreams of who-knows-what while both cheeks boof in and out like an inverted bagpipe. This makes me smile. I'm not advocating anarchy—rules matter. If I'd prefer DJ not swipe my scrunchy, I would tell him so and that would be that. Likewise, I can readily call Buddha off the couch. With a little finesse, it's possible to have it all.

Over-Thinking Imp

Ever hear the expression, "Don't believe everything you think"? I'm not sure who coined it, but it sure makes sense when rearing a puppy. Don't get me wrong; I think thinking is a good thing. And I like to think that I, too, am a thinker. Perfectionistic Over-Thinking, however, often does more harm than good.

I have counseled countless confused clients who did or didn't do this or that because they "thought" they should (or shouldn't)—like there's a law. Some Over-Thinkers obsess over particulars: "I thought I was supposed to say Wait not Stay," or "Eh! instead of No!" I explain that timing and intonation matter more than word choice. If the Over-Thinker challenges this, I turn to Imp and in my sing-songiest voice coo, "You are the ugliest, dumbest dog in the whole wide world!" Ten to one, Imp responds with a slobbery, "Thank you very much."

A more insidious conflict for Over-Thinkers is withholding comfort to a frightened or lonely puppy lest it promotes future attention-seeking behaviors. These people often admit that doing so felt wrong but did it anyway because they "thought" they were supposed to. And it's true, over-coddling conveys the wrong message but less damagingly than totally ignoring or reprimanding distraught Imp.

Behavior modification is a fluid process that's part art, part science: more pluses and minuses than black and white. Calm reassurance is a compassionate compromise that demonstrates your trustworthiness. This may not always get the desired result but at least it will do no harm that requires future fixing. If your head and your heart disagree, please follow your heart. That is a decidedly dog thing to do.

What a Difference a Dog Makes

Dogs stink, most shed and they cost a fortune to feed. Dogs jump, chew and bark, and their urine yellows the lawn. Dogs have to be walked Sunday mornings even in the rain. And where do you put them when you're away?

Then there's the face factor, a phenomenon so teeth-crunchingly irresistible you'll recognize it the second you see it. Puppy breath is intoxicating—stroking their fur, health affirming. Dogs get you out of the house when you're blue and make you laugh so hard that fluids squirt out of orifices they oughtn't. If you don't get what a difference a dog makes, please don't get a dog.

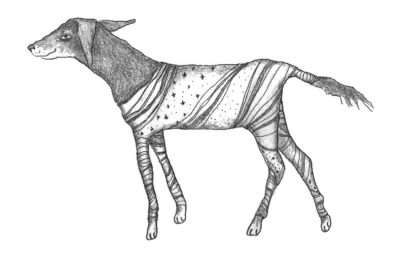

CHAPTER 2

ImPerfect Puppy Selection Grownup Dogs, Too

Perfectionistic Puppy Selection is a crazy-making process. Some people obsess over selection with little thought to what happens next, much like obsessing over the wedding with little consideration for the marriage.

I will never forget Richard, a Wall Street analyst, who boasted having spent three years researching over one hundred potential breeds—foreign and domestic—before finally selecting "the Perfect" one, a Swiss Mountain Dog, that met 90% of his criteria. I bet you can guess where this story is going: Igor was dumped in four months.

Then there was Brigit who flew to her native Norway to purchase an eight-week-old Elkhound whom she promptly tied to a pole on her deck in 90+ degrees humid heat his first day home while she napped. A neighbor's call to Animal Control in response to the puppy's cries is all that saved his life.

Dogs are no more Perfect than the rest of us, so look for a breed or mix whose imperfections you can most easily live with by first assessing size, temperament, trainability, exercise and grooming requirements.

I'm okay with shedding but can't bear a yapper. Apparently the same was true for the lawyer who called to ask what I thought of Shetland Sheepdogs. After itemizing Shelties' many virtues, I mentioned that they are rather barky. "Fine," he said, "so I'll hire you to teach him not to bark." "But," answered I, "that's like marrying a flat-chested brunette with the intention of transforming her into a buxom blond." I later found out that that's exactly what he did. Perhaps this is a better illustration of the control freak, a subdivision of Perfectionism.

I've always rescued mutts—or as I prefer, "multiple-pedigrees"—but I don't judge people who do not. Adopting them makes me feel good about myself. And I don't like someone less for preferring a puppy to a mature dog, pedigree vs. mixed-breed or a small dog over a large one. Dog parenting is too huge a commitment to be guilt-tripped into. Nowhere is it written that you even have to have a dog. However, it is written (here) that if you so choose, you must do right by them, which brings us back to Selection.

Puppy vs. Adult

The benefit of adopting a puppy is that you can mold one from scratch. The down side is that puppies are a ton of work. The advantage of adopting an adult dog is that more are in need of a home and, with most, you won't be as tied down as with a pup. The downside to an older dog is inheriting someone else's issues and many develop Separation Anxiety. This will be discussed on page 51 in "Remedies For The Rescued Dog."

Pure vs. Mixed-Breed

With a pedigreed dog you know what you're getting and with a mix you may not. Mutts tend to be heartier and they're awfully adorable.

Male vs. Female

Because I believe in spaying and neutering all companion dogs, the behavioral extremes are narrower than in those who are intact. I have observed a strong opposite sex preference from a pup to his or her people. In a heavily male-dominant home, I'd get a female, and vice versa.

CHAPTER 3

Locating Your
Good Enough Pup

C ommon sense dictates seeking personal referrals and staying close to home. If finding a local pup is not possible, the Internet is an amazing resource but, with so many choices, it's a fertile breeding ground for Perfectionistic Paralysis. Another problem with the Web is it makes locating a far away pup so simple that dogs are being shipped all over the globe like grapefruit, which has got to be traumatic for the poor creature, begging the question: can you really only love an Imp from Azerbaijan?

Mixed-Breeds

Most Mixed-Breed lovers are less Perfectionistic than their purebred counterparts; so first check your local shelters. There is a trend these days to truck Mixed-Breeds, and even some pedigrees, from areas where they're not wanted to areas that they are, win-winningly. My own Cozy and Doc hail from the South. Most of these dogs are found through rescue groups on the Internet and often end up at local shelters or at Adoptathons. Some groups will even drive the pup to your house.

Pedigrees

Breeders

Dog Breeders are amongst the most controlling people on earth and will insist that their dogs are of higher "quality" than everyone else's. This breed of elitism brings out the Tramp in me. Because Breeders create and sometimes "cull" life for a living, many possess a Godlike belief that they alone are expert on everything puppy, including which one is "perfect" for you, prohibiting interaction with the litter. And God forbid you have a problem with the puppy's health or behavior down the line, be prepared to hear, "This never happened before so it's obviously all your fault!" I've known many prospective customers who were so intimidated by bully Breeders that they fled into a Pet Shop's welcoming arms. Clearly there are honorable Breeders out there whose knowledge of each puppy's temperament is an invaluable asset in the selection process. By abandoning your own need for the Perfect Pup, I am confident you'll find such a Breeder.

Heads Up! Breeders commonly sell Show Dogs who, for behavioral, medical and visual reasons, don't make the grade. That these dogs were selectively bred and reared for this narrow existence leaves many ill-equipped to cope as companions. Because it's impossible to know which dogs will and won't pan out, I strongly encourage Breeders to also socialize them for this eventuality.

Pet Shops

After so many *exposés*, I am appalled that otherwise intelligent people still buy puppies in Pet Shops where they are merchandised like appliances and impulse acquisitions are the name of the game. If a pup's appeal grows stale from hanging around too long, he'll get marked down like a day-old bagel. No matter how persuasively storekeepers doth protests that their puppies are not from Puppy Mills—they are. No self-respecting breeder would dump their dogs there. Papers prove nothing; even assembly line puppies have them. And please don't deceive yourself into believing that by buying a puppy from a Pet Shop you're "rescuing it." You're not. That puppy will be replaced before his cage gets cold.

Breed-Specific Rescue Leagues

On a brighter note, in case you don't already know, most breeds can be adopted through Rescue Leagues. This way you can save a dog and know what you're getting. These are usually adult dogs, though I have heard of an occasional puppy being available. As enthusiastically as I support going this route, don't do so if your sole motivation is to save on the sticker price. Rehomed dogs often need medical or behavioral intervention that will eat-up the savings. Another reason not to adopt an adult pure or mixed-breed is the presumption he's housebroken. Being old enough to know better doesn't mean one does.

CHAPTER 4

How To Select Your Good Enough Pup

I adopted each of my current dogs sight unseen because I like a challenge and knew that, short of their channeling Cujo, I was committed to keeping them no matter what. But that's me. For most of you, a more systematic search is probably preferable.

Ideally, visit the Shelter* or breeder three times at different times of day before picking your Imp (but no more than three you Perfectionists, you). The puppy that appears most mellow at first blush may have just trampled his littermates and is simply refueling before the next assault, while Mr. Manic is actually only enjoying a momentary energy surge upon awakening from a four-hour nap. I'd advise against selecting a pup at the extremes of behavior, especially if you have young children. Charming though the little bruiser or shy pup cowering in the corner might be, he can be a handful. Adult dogs' behavior is more stable, so multiple visits aren't as important.

I have adopted infant puppies and mature strays of indeterminate ages. I have adopted mixed and purebreds, some who were lovingly reared and others who had been brutally abused, and I am constantly astonished by a dog's resiliency. In abandoning the myth of Perfection an opening is made for your heart's content to enter. That you extrapolate this to other relationships is fine with me.

* For brevity's sake, Shelter also includes dogs in foster care and elsewhere.

Déjà vu (DJ) Dog and Ernie Bird

I love German shepherds and drove sixteen-hours round trip to Lake Placid to adopt what I was told was a German shepherd-mix puppy from friends who paid the drunk trying to drown him $20. After 45-minutes of sweet-talking and Swiss cheese, I finally coaxed what looked like a Yellow Lab out from beneath the porch. As my heart sank but, not wanting to seem superficial or like an ingrate, I feigned delight while calculating how I could unload this non-German Shepherd.

Don't get me wrong, some of my best friends are Labrador Retrievers, it's just that I wouldn't have traveled that far to get one who, being so devastatingly handsome, would have been adopted locally in a heartbeat. To make matters worse, one hour into the ride home it became apparent that the puppy was very sick. After $1200 of work-ups, the third vet I brought DJ to that first week diagnosed him with a rare disease for which he'd need twice-daily injections of an obscenely expensive medicine for life, saddling me with a sickly puppy I didn't want to begin with because—let's face it— who'd adopt a mutt with a pricey drug habit? You guessed it; DJ became the unequalled love of my life.

Ernie Bird is a Senegal parrot who was twenty-two when I adopted him. Having five other adopted parrots, I decided to take on one more because I had a hankering (and a spare cage) and I specifically asked for a difficult-to-adopt bird. The rescuer told me she had a special soul who was sweet as could be not much to look at so adopters didn't give him the time of day. I raced one hundred miles, bypassed strapping blue and gold and scarlet birds, to meet crumpled little half-bald Ernie Bird with a wheeze and instantly wanted to back out of taking him while still saving face. Ernie Bird is now Johnny Depp to me.

Sidebar: Please know that I loathe the caging of animals, especially birds. I adopted each of the present and past parrots when relinquished by their caretakers or following their deaths. Because parrots live so long, captive birds average five homes in their lifetime. It pains me deeply that my brood can't fly free in its native habitat. With that ship having sailed, I work very hard to ensure their life here, though ImPerfect, is as good as can be.

CHAPTER 5

Homecoming

Ideally, bring Imp home as early in the day as possible at the beginning of a long weekend or school vacation. This is a monumental day for all the players so you want everyone to be as settled as possible before bedtime.

Making A Good Enough First ImPression

In advance of Imp's homecoming, think through the pup's domain: which room(s) he will and will not have access to, the door(s) you'll take him out through, have a crate, baby gate(s), food, toys, a No Chew spray, and allow incoming Imp to investigate his puppy proofed turf, unfettered, for as long as it takes to get his bearings. Roughly the same amount of a dog's brain is devoted to scent as a human's is to sight. 80% of what we learn is through our eyes. So, if A=B and B=C then Imp needs to inhale his new digs to feel safe.

Imp-Proofing

Some people Puppy Proof their homes within an inch of its life, while others do nothing to accommodate Imp. I vote for something in-between.

Because I share a crowded cottage with a lot of large animals, I'm currently keeping infant Cozy out of the parrots' Wing as there's lots in there that could hurt her, including the parrots. I've also cordoned off the half of the living room with the good stuff and Puppy Proofed the remaining three rooms and the basement so we can co-exist with some semblance of normalcy. I'd get cranky if the house felt too sterile, and claustrophobic if I couldn't move about without crashing into a gate.

If you live in a huge house with one little dog—or even a big one—I think it's fine to permanently keep certain rooms off limits. Why not? However, it's important to introduce Imp to the rooms that he'll ultimately have access to from the get-go. I take Cozy into The Wing and the good half of the living room daily to ensure they're not too forbidden-fruity when I dispense with the barriers. People often wait until the pup's 100% housebroken in the kitchen to permit access to the rest of the house, assuming that the terms will be generalized elsewhere. However, if the only time Imp ever leaves the kitchen is to go outdoors, he may think that all doors out of the kitchen lead to the loo.

Of course you'll be supervising Imp in the formal dining room and intervene if he's about to pee or chew the drapes. To make for a more relaxed outing, remove what's portable like wicker baskets and houseplants and pre-spray the irresistible fringe of oriental rugs, *armoire* corners and computer cables with your No Chew product to convey that it is never kosher to nosh here. Puppies LOVE fringe, corners and cables.

And be prepared to regroup until you get it right. If stationing Imp in the northeast corner of the kitchen proves too sunny or chaotic, the southwest side of the den will do. As long as you are emotionally consistent, there's a lot of logistical wiggle room.

Back in my hippy days, Algunza, a pregnant German Shepherd I found as a college freshman, traveled the country with my musician boyfriend and me. I sold vegetarian tacos out of our VW Van by day while Bob gigged at night and Algunza was the most chilled dog you'd ever want to meet. I was her constant. Those days are long gone and my current brood of four dogs and six parrots live a more conventional existence. Being a single freelancer, our schedule varies within a range that they accept as their norm. My adult dogs expect dinner when I get home, whether at 4:00 or 7:00, and they know that after an hour with the New York Times crossword puzzle, a Sunday morning walk is in order. Baby Cozy's biological needs to eat, sleep, pee and poop require more structure, but we're only talking a few months of such intense specificity.

Please don't worry that you'll ruin Imp if you don't get everything Perfect right off the bat. A first-time prospective dog Ma has called and emailed eighteen times over the past two months about a puppy who has yet to be born. So nervous is this woman that she'll make a mistake, she's already booked me weekly starting with the pup's presumptive arrival date. I explained that, despite all I know about animals, I constantly make adjustments with a new family member until I arrive upon the recipe that's right. Dogs are big-hearted souls who have endured for 100,000 years as the most adaptable animals on the planet by seeing the forest for the trees of our intentions. Besides, it's all the worrying that wounds. Here's what I mean:

Dogs don't differentiate our negative emotions. Nor can they distinguish our fear, anger, worry, guilt, etc. as being *for* them versus *at* them. Rather, all this negativity gets jumbled up into an olio of despair from which individual dogs respond in whatever way they are predisposed.

Fight, Flight and Freeze

This is a good time to discuss Fight, Flight and their lesser-known relation, Freeze. We are all wired to respond to feeling threatened by Fighting, Fleeing or Freezing. Which option one exercises first is a function of both nature and nurture, making for a dizzying flurry of combinations.

Let's say baby Imp and you are strolling around the 'hood and you're worried that the Boxer heading your way will scare him. In response to your perfuse perspiration and halting gait, fearful Imp tries to flee from the offender while bold Imp wants to take him out. Of course the opposite is also true. By communicating that the burly Boxer makes you ever so happy, Imp will respond in kind. I've sold all sorts of crap to dogs over the years, including DJ's injections, by acting like they're a blessed thing. And if you're wondering what happened to Freeze, this is when Imp gets stark still as if holding his breath with the intention of saying, "Walk on by." If Freeze's subtlety is not recognized, Fight or Flight follows.

Dogs are non-sequential learners with a different sense of timing than ours, almost like a separate system. We view the flip cards as a continuous cartoon; dogs focus on each frame. Boxer approaches; Ma's a mess. Boxer departs; Ma relaxes. Whether positive or negative, intended or inadvertent, dogs connect reinforcement to the closest event. If a bee stings Imp as the Boxer emerges an opposite reaction will be elicited than your offering a liver bit. Some estimate the lag time to be as tight as thirty seconds, though I'm not convinced, besides, dogs aren't uniformly responsive. Still, the closer the reinforcement to the event, the better.

Many people interpret the immediacy with which dogs learn as proof that they have no memory. Tell that to the twelve-year-old Cocker Spaniel, Luna, whose house I returned to after eleven years because her folks brought home a ne'er-do-well Dalmatian puppy. Spotting me, Luna piddled and whimpered and dug out the stuffed Santa I had given her in

her youth to parade it in front of the pup who wondered what was so wonderful about me, anyway.

Those who believe dogs have no memory also think they're incapable of predicting future events. Really? Ten to one I jiggle my car keys and four mutts bolt to the back door. The point isn't that dogs exclusively live in the present so much as that's where they learn. Dogs don't ruminate over last week's transgressions, nor can they be dissuaded from chewing your Vera Wangs today with a promissory trip to FAO Schwartz tomorrow.

As straightforwardly as I present Imp's sense of timing, I cannot tell you how often a client challenges it. A regular "yeah but" goes something like, "So how come when I return home the dog looks guilty and then hides from me if he's taken a dump, huh?" To which I say something like, "I suspect that, because you punished Imp for prior mistakes upon coming home, he is now scared of you and he would have hidden even if he hadn't pooped. Besides, dreading you might be why he unloaded to begin with." Checkmate.

Entertaining Imp

I don't know what it's like where you live, but around here there's a lot of Type A Puppy Parenting going on. These folks frequently complain that they can't "play with" infant Imp because of his incessant "biting."

I met one such family earlier whose Pointer puppy, Rupert, was so exhausted he reminded me of a dozing subway rider struggling to hold his head upright. In response to the family's non-stop handling and bossing Rupert about, the pup's biting—or as I prefer, "mouthing"—was a desperate plea to be left alone. The more they pestered, the more intensely he protested. When I mentioned this, Ma said she thought they were supposed to "poop Rupert out." And it is true that a tired puppy is a peaceful puppy. It is also true that there's a colossal chasm between tired and fried.

Overstimulation and understimulation are the two main reasons Imp gets into trouble. Understimulation is an obvious cause for concern. What's less obvious, though, is that never leaving him alone is also problematical.

After hearing the robust regimen these Type A-ers employed with infant Imp that would have overwhelmed many a mature dog, I reminded them that Rupert's been on this earth for all of ten weeks. While no parent would expect her toddler to run a marathon, I suspect that a puppy's looking just like a miniaturized grownup contributes to the confusion.

Ma then asked how they should play with Rupert and I answered, "They shouldn't." More often than not, "play with" is code for roughhousing, which results in Imp's being overstimulated and the person getting hurt. And if that person is a child, an easily avoidable conflict can spiral out of control fast.

Our job is to educate and socialize Imp so we can safely exercise him through walking, jogging, Frisbee, retrieving, agility, tracking, swimming or whatever you both agree upon. And when it's time to take a break from all the Entertaining, redirect Imp to a passive, long-lasting solitary pursuit. Like transitioning from playing ping-pong with Junior to turning on a movie, simply hand Imp a dog-safe bone before he becomes totally unglued. Now leave him alone to chew it instead of you.

Buyer's Remorse

I just visited a couple that I've helped with three prior dogs over a twenty-year stretch and I consider them very dog savvy. The past dogs were adult rescues and they just brought home their first puppy and, well, it wasn't pretty.

Alma is a high school principal used to jogging before work, and Warren is an avid tennis-playing accountant. Neither anticipated giving anything up to accommodate baby Jackson. I explained that it is possible to exercise and be puppy parents but perhaps they'd need to sleep a little less or shampoo every other day or eat instant oatmeal instead of the good stuff for a while. I know this seems like a Duh! but I am often surprised by otherwise intelligent people's *un*common sense.

Post-Puppy Depression

On Cozy's fourth day here I woke up feeling overwhelmed and anxious, certain that adopting her was the biggest mistake of my life. Then I got all rah-rah and reminded myself that I suffered Post-Puppy Depression following every adoption and that the intensity is short-lived and that I do this for a living so get a grip, already! That's when I noticed that Cozy had sprung her crate and was sound asleep in my underwear drawer with her head threaded through a thong. The sun set in the west again.

A Few Odds and Ends While I Think of Them

1. If you were told to Ferberize infant Imp if he whimpers those first few nights, please don't. By Ferberize, I mean allowing Imp to cry himself to sleep; the premise being that acknowledgement reinforces the crying thereby ensuring its continuance. While this is conceptually sound, I believe it's contextually inappropriate. There is a huge difference between reassurance and reinforcement, with the former being compassionate and the latter being cruel.

   Cozy sleeps in a crate next to my bed and she whined intermittently for the first three nights as if to ask, "Where am I, again?" With each awakening I stayed in bed, dangled my fingers in the cage while calmly saying, "I'm right here, go back to sleep." And she did. Making a big to-do might have taught her to seek the attention, whereas I couldn't have lived with myself had I ignored her altogether.

   If Imp sleeps in a separate room, offer reassurance through an intercom or even sleep in the den with him for a few nights. True, this could make returning to your bedroom painful, but I have known hundreds of puppies who, once secure in their new digs, readily accept sleeping solo. Hopefully, you will recover equally well.

2. Ever see Andrew Wyeth's painting, Master Bedroom, with the yellow dog asleep on the bed as though to absorb his Master? Every dog I've ever known would, if they could, do the same. To ensure Imp is as secure as possible, and to hasten your bonding, provide him with a used sheet, blanket or towel stuffed in a pillowcase all of which reek of you. Now that Imp's security blankey is identified and enjoyed, take it with the two of you on vacation or to a barbecue.

3. Dogs don't care about *décor*. Cozy had been hospitalized for three days with pneumonia prior to my bringing her home when we were in the midst of an unprecedented cold snap so I couldn't take her outdoors. In need of romping room, I converted my crude cellar into a playground with its own indoor plumbing. Cozy colored this Disney World.

4. You may have been told that all dogs love their crate. I wish. Many do, some don't. Just as Junior isn't required to adore his crib, Imp simply has to tolerate the crate to use it. For pups who are especially resistant to the crate, try a little reverse psychology by packing it with primo snacks and lock Imp out. I did this with baby Buddha who soon pleaded "pretty please" for the privilege of being admitted.

Heads up! Some dogs with Separation Anxiety, or those who were traumatized during transport, panic and react violently to being crated. This was the case with Doc. Here, find another means of containment as discussed on page 57 in "Safely Containing Anxious Imp Sans Crate."

5. To keep Imp out of a room temporarily where gates won't work, create an inexpensive, short term barrier by placing duct tape strips across the open doorway. Hedge your bet by spritzing a little No Chew Spray on the tape. I'd first try this with the non-sticky side facing Imp to avoid spooking Imp. However, with a bold pup, go ahead and reverse the tape. It will do no harm while being creepy enough to be avoided. And it case you haven't seen, these

tapes now come in all sorts of bold colors, designs and thicknesses, so color this makeshift barrier a fashion statement.

6. Most dogs care more about proximity to their people than square footage. If asked whether they'd prefer to accompany me on errands in my cramped Honda or to stay home on two acres, three-quarters of my dogs would vote for the former.

A retired couple whose mansion was so immense that they bickered over whether there were nine or ten bedrooms, hired me to help with their Labrador Retriever's anxiety that reduced her to a drooling, gas-passing mess. They adopted Molly through the Guiding Eyes for The Blind in Yorktown Heights, NY after she was released from the program for being, "excessively sensitive."

The Smiths installed a state-of-the-art kennel with state-of-the-art dog door so Molly had access to the five-car garage and a Hidden Fence enclosed all twelve acres. The "help" fed Molly premium food and their vet paid house calls, but the Smiths barely interacted with the dog. While we sipped tea in the sunroom pondering Molly's rehabilitation as she lay outside the sliding door looking in longingly, I suggested we invite her to join us, reminding them that Molly had been selectively bred and conditioned to be close to her blind person. Once inside, Molly curled up beneath my chair, draped her head across my feet. This is where she slept for two hours with nary a toot.

Chapter 6

Now What?

Housebreaking and Basic Training will be discussed, in depth, in subsequent chapters. Here are some broad-stroke expectations and suggestions.

Timeline

Whether you buy an eight-week-old puppy or adopt an eight-year-old dog, Imp will be in shock for the first four days and he'll begin to thaw by day five. Between ten to fourteen days his true colors emerge, and at six weeks you're finishing each other's sentences.

By virtue of Imp's condensed lifespan, puppies sprint through each developmental phase, often in weeks, so finding a serviceable hurry-up-and-wait formula is challenging. There's contradictory data about the developmental phases, and because you'll be getting dogs of all ages, here's a Good Enough priority checklist.

The Orientation Period

Whatever Imp's age, for those first two weeks, demonstrate through calm consistency that yours is a safe, predictable environment. Imp needs to know that food, water, shelter, toys, affection, exercise and down time will be provided. This is when he learns that the family is trustworthy, so it's best not to invite shifty old Uncle Rudy over. Kudos if you've cleared time to be around more than usual, but please don't make the mistake of never leaving Imp alone, just do so briefly. If in doubt about how strict to be at first, lean towards leniency. There's time to tighten the reigns anon. I don't believe it's possible to spoil incoming Imp with compassion.

A prospective client called to say she was adopting a two-year-old Bernese Mountain Dog who was being driven six hours by his heartbroken person in failing health who could no longer care for Alpine. The caller went on to say that she intended to show the dog who's "alpha" upon his arrival by not touching or talking to him or allowing him out of the car until he sat and that she'd withhold water until he learned where to pee. She seemed to think this would impress me. Alpine was rehomed before our first scheduled session the following week.

Between Two and Three Months

Eight weeks is a common age for puppies to be brought home, so this is where our timeline will begin.

Puppies don't have sphincter muscle control before three months, so take infant Imp to his designated toilet often with the intention of getting lucky a lot. Mid-squat say something like, "Hurry up" so he'll ultimately connect the word with what he is out there to do. Imp may tinkle multiple times per outing, especially the first one of the day, so stay out long enough for him to empty. And wait until he stands upright to praise lest he stops midway to receive your, "Atta Imp!" Enthusiastically praise a well-placed puddle or pile, but don't correct mistakes at this point, simply clean them up. It's fine to sometimes rush him back into the house, don't always do so. The outdoors is more than an outhouse to Imp and you don't want to inadvertently teach him to delay relieving himself to hang outside longer. And when it is time to head inside, say something like, "Go home."

Also begin labeling desirable behaviors Imp spontaneously performs so you can eventually request them without formal tutelage. When he charges towards you, sweetly say, "Come!" As his baby butt hits the dirt say, "Sit," etc. By connecting freely offered behaviors to words, language is organically learned. And if—make that when—you pry contraband out of Imp's mouth, calmly say, "Drop " so this is understood before his vice-like jaw gains its grip. The significance of sounding nonchalant is to convey that your request is no big deal. To sound anxious gives the event too much weight, potentially ramping-up a proportionate response on Imp's part. By the way, if you'd rather say, "Give" or "Release" instead of "Drop," be my guest. In Guadalajara dogs learn to *sientese* in Espanol.

Tenderly touch Imp all over while placing extra emphasis on the mouth, ears, feet and tail, as these are potential problem spots. If his coat will require frequent brushing, buy a soft baby brush and, using the backside if necessary for desensitization purposes, get him used to the action, albeit briefly, even if you don't actually accomplish much. To soothe a squirmy puppy, exert a fair amount of pressure on his chest with your fingers tips while rubbing tight little circles.

I understand how absolutely irresistible lifting a brand-spanking-new puppy is, but if Imp is going to grow into a gorilla, carry him sparingly as your ability to do so is short-lived. To help him relax in your arms, try cupping his rear feet with one hand while supporting his chest with the other. And if he'll stay small, please remember he does have feet. Even a pocket-sized pooch will go postal if he never gets to tree a squirrel.

> *Sidebar: Infant Imps sleep a lot. This can be unbearable for kids who anticipated getting a puppy for their whole entire lives and now all the dumb dog does is sleep! Please explain that Imp will grow up fast and will then need less sleep but if they wake him up now he'll be a big fat doody-head. I'm guessing the person who coined "Let sleeping dogs lie" knew this.*

Three to Four Months

Once Imp learns the lay of the land, mix things up a bit. Who needs an uptight dog that can't go with the flow?

Thanksgiving morning a distraught client phoned because her four-month-old Tibetan Terrier still peed in the living room and company was due in an hour. When I suggested that she gate off the living room until we could discuss this at a more appropriate time, my psychologist client said, "But Sigmund's too set in his ways." Sigmund's too set in *his* ways? I think not.

I read somewhere that a dog's biological clock is accurate within thirty-seconds in a twenty-four-hour period—and I can attest that every puppy I've ever raised has overslept by an hour at Daylight Savings Time—so start altering Imp's routine in twenty minute increments. Twenty minutes seems an important timeframe, though I couldn't tell you why. Begin to push his staying home alone muscle in twenty-minute increments as well.

Time to add stressors. Drop a book on the floor or slam the door. Remember, Imp takes his cues from you so, by acting *blasé* about the commotion, you convey the insignificance of loud noises. Gently step on Imp's foot and casually apologize. Go ahead and invite Uncle Rudy over.

Sidebar: Some dramatic dogs develop Sympathetic Lameness, a psychosomatic attention-seeking limp. My Mowgli hurt his foot early on in our relationship. Until the day he died fourteen years later, Mowgli became ever so lame whenever we had words, often switching limbs mid-limp.

Introduce Imp to puppies and adult dogs as soon as it is safe to do so. Here's where age matters. With youngsters, follow your veterinarian's recommendation, vaccination-wise. Different parts of the country are susceptible to different diseases that can mutate. I used to be cavalier about communicative diseases until my newly adopted puppy, Drummer, died of the Parvovirus twelve years ago.

Please know that it is rare for an adult dog to harm a puppy, though it does happen. Mostly, grown-ups find an in-your-face Imp irritating and give them a warning what-for. It is also rare for dogs of the opposite sex to fight, though that, too, has happened. While I advocate *laissez-faire* introductions amongst dogs of similar age and heft, I wouldn't seat a geriatric Newfoundland on the other end of young Toto's teeter-totter.

Four to Six Months

Can you imagine anything worse than a teething teenager? Me either, but that's what happens between four and six months. What was Mother Nature thinking?

Puppies are born toothless and immediately grow those sharp little milk teeth that begin falling out around four-months and by six-months they've spawned a whole second set of monster choppers. This timing is pretty fixed. Less certain is when those heady hormones kick in, but it could coincide. And to totally muck-up the works, pubescent Imp hits the Flight Phase around five-months. Like his teenaged human counterpart, Imp is programmed to individuate himself by pushing boundaries. No longer is he happy to stay home Saturday night and play Scrabble with the family, Imp's now hitting you up for the car keys.

The Flight Phase is especially worrisome because unsuspecting dog parents get lulled into a false sense of security and think that, because infant Imp had hung around faithfully, he's still safe without a leash or fence and now take lethal risks.

Here's where it helps to understand a little wolf behavior. Dogs are domesticated wolves. This is easy to envision in a Siberian Husky but a Pug? Still, dogs and wolves can mate and have viable offspring so they must be the same. We share 98.6% of our DNA with Bonobo chimpanzees—which is a lot of DNA—but we are too distant for hybridization. Wild canines usually mate in March so, with nine-weeks gestation, their pups are born in May to maximize access to warmth, prey, and daylight. The Flight Phase is therefore most pronounced if Imp turns five-months in the spring.

Ideally, the minute Imp hits the Flight Phase he'll meander next-door and get spooked by Uncle Rudy or a feral cat or a car's backfiring and be so traumatized as to never stray again. It may even be worth safely setting up such a scenario while also enriching Imp's home turf with toys and treats to demonstrate that "there's no place like home."

Four to six months is the heart and soul of well-rounded Imp's formal education. Go all out with Basic Training (see page 69) now that he's mature enough to get it and there's little to undo. Expose Imp to as much variety as you can conjure with the objective of making these pleasant experiences so he won't be leery of them later. If you live in the city, introduce Imp to a moose. Take the suburban dog downtown. Travel a lot? Schedule a quick weekend trip so Imp gets used to the kennel or sitter prior to leaving him in earnest for the Galapagos. And if you intend to take Imp on vacation, plan a test overnight prior to checking into a B&B for two weeks. It's time to schedule Imp's neutering. If you intend to use a hidden "Invisible" type fence, plan Imp's training to be at least two weeks before or after surgery.

Six Months to One Year

By six months, the armature of Imp's life with you should be built so the next six months are about filling-in the connective tissue. While Imp had been the center of your world, adjust the amount of attention given him for long-term endurance, like transitioning from a sprint to marathon running. He's no longer the "new" kid; he's just the kid. Many pups go through a chewing regression around ten-months so, even if Imp had proven trustworthy earlier, don't dispense with the crate yet as it will be difficult to reintroduce once he's comfy in his big boy bed.

Customize the pup's schooling to accommodate your specific lifestyle and needs. Outfit nautical Imp with a lifejacket and take him out on your catamaran. Love to entertain? It's foolhardy to assume Imp will be well-mannered at your cocktail party. Rather than wait until the bowl is half-empty to teach him not to lap the dip, rehearse etiquette up-front. I know you're busy and role-playing with *crudités* seems silly but, just as you wouldn't wait until your daughter stops breathing to learn CPR, had that dip been a bowl of raisins, Imp's devouring it would have killed him. (Common toxins will be mentioned under Chewing on pages 93-94.)

One Year and Beyond

While fine-tuning your pictured life with Imp, remember he also has aspirations of his own. Even if you dreamt he'd grow up to be a master chef, I'd be grateful if he becomes a law-abiding bus boy. Between ten and eighteen months, territoriality rears its head in those dogs so inclined. By two, you know the dog you've got so it's safe to introduce Impette #2.

Adopting a Mature Dog

Much of the above is applicable to the older adoptee with the notable difference that you've missed key developmental markers, and even the easiest adoptee has a history. Imp may have been permitted on the furniture in his first home but this is unacceptable to you, or he lived on two fenced acres and you're in a condo, or his last family fed him from the table but this makes your skin crawl. These lifestyle differences ought not be a deal breaker—Good Enough fixes exist. Rehomed Imp's tendency towards Separation Anxiety is a big deal that will be addressed, in-depth, on page 51 in "Remedies for the Rescued Dog."

Finally, there are many ways to build your Good Enough pup. My home life is rather solitary so I want Cozy to be receptive and appropriate with guests, but I need her to be comfortable living with nine other critters and a single parent. If yours is a social household, conditioning your pup to navigate around the action will serve you. I admire independence and foster it in all my relationships. The micromanager might require tighter oversight.

Watching my dogs race through the woods, unbridled, stopping to sip from a stream or to play keep-away with the only worthwhile stick in the forest, fills me with such joy that, within bounds, I leave them alone to find their way. The bounds of our individual threshold vary vastly. I adore cuddling with my guys in bed but I'm intolerant of begging. You might feel the opposite. As long as these lifestyle decisions are victimless, I would never presume to advise.

CHAPTER 7

A Whole Lot of Dog Talking Going On

E ven as we speak, dogs and people all over the world are doing terrible things to one another because each misunderstands what the other one is saying. Intonation and timing are the main mistakes we make that confuse Imp. Examples of each are woven through the text. Here is some Dog Talk we frequently misinterpret.

Tail Wagging

People typically assume that a wagging tail is always friendly. And it's true, a sweeping horizontal tail wag communicates "life is good," but a low, slow, between-the-legs wag says, "I'm scared to death," and a high wag with only the tip moving cautions, "Back off, Jack!" whereas a high, whole tail wag either advertises Imp's dominant status or that he's feeling amorous or even his euphoria over dispatching an opossum. Many terrier tails are perpetually erect making them, and the lopped off tails of some breeds, impossible to read. With so many dialects, if in doubt about what a tail is saying, I wouldn't touch.

Grumbles vs. Growls

Because they're both guttural utterances, Grumbles and Growls are easy to confuse. What I call a Grumble is happy, full-bodied and wavery, almost like a yodel that accompanies relaxed body language. A Growl emanates from deep in the throat and is quieter and more level than a Grumble. Growling Imp is quite still, as if holding his breath. When resource guarding, his neck turtles out slightly led by the chin. Where there's a devil-may-care quality to a Grumble, a Growl has no sense of humor. Grumbles are intended to engage but Growls say, "Make my day." Mishandled, Grumbles easily evolve into a Growl.

I paid a house call to evaluate a newly adopted Minpin's "extreme aggression" as evidenced by her frequent "growling." A few minutes into the session, Angel crooned a, "Wanna play?" Grumble that was harshly rebuked by both parents. Defensive, Angel stiffened and eventually did Growl in response to the finger that wagged menacingly in her face, a causal relationship that eluded Ma and Pa. So I waited for Angel to Grumble again and asked her to sit before tossing a stuffed rooster that she chased with utter glee. This was repeated dozens of times throughout our 90-minute, snarl-free session.

Raised Hackles (Piloerection)

Talk about misunderstood! Despite popular opinion, hair raised along Imp's neck or spine is rarely a sign of aggression. Like goose bumps or blushing, piloerection is an involuntary response to arousal, with confusion and fear being very arousing. Cozy's fur shoots up like Alphalfa's when encountering anything new. With each episode averaging fifteen seconds, I simply wait for Cozy to get a grip and then extol her relaxing.

Smiling

There's nothing I get a bigger kick out of than a Smiling dog. This is when the odd Imp bears his teeth while lovingly saying hello or to appease.

Smiling is so rare and atypical that most people assume grinning Imp is about to take their face off. My ReRun, a 105-pound German Shepherd-mix, was a huge Smiler. Being greeted by a flash of ReRun's beefy fangs caused many a heart-stopping moment. Dogs don't Smile at food or toys or chipmunks or other dogs, they only Smile at us, as if mimicking a uniquely human behavior for which there is no canid precedent. To make sure you're not misreading a Smile, look at Imp's total body language. If threatening, he's rigid and erect; if Smiling, he's loose and at ease. The scrunched upper lip of a prolonged Smile might tickle Imp's nose, so also listen for a sneeze.

The Play Bow

For the life of me, I can't figure out how people misread this, but many do. If Imp's front end is stooped and his rear's raised with tail wagging wildly, he's saying, "Let's play!" This stance is so cut-and-dry that you, too, could easily invite Imp to par-tay by wagging your own rump from bended knee.

The Pronated Wrist

Ever notice Imp Pronate (fold) his wrist while lying down? Some supple dogs can even fold both wrists as if praying. Whether Imp is at the vet, dog class or has houseguests, his at ease wrist is always a good sign that says, "All is well in the world." The Pronated wrist is involuntary and need not be present for Imp to be relaxed. When working with dogs who have a biting history, once I see that folded wrist I, too, am at ease.

How Dogs Play Amongst Themselves

Without a doubt, a person's #1 most misunderstood dog behavior is how they play, so let me set the record straight: Dogs Play by chasing, chomping, jumping, tugging and sucking face with one another. Raised hackles, bared teeth and grumbles accompany most Dog Play. Like a tennis player's grunts or a partner's groaning during s.e.x, these are happy sounds so please don't knock on the door.

CHAPTER 8

All About Rescued Dogs

The demographics of my practice have changed dramatically over the past few years with Rescued Dogs equaling Pedigrees purchased as puppies. While this thrills me, a new set of issues has arisen that now needs addressing.

By Rescued, I mean a stray or one adopted from a shelter, adoption group or individual who gave up on him or one taken from an abusive home.

Strays

A common scenario in many parts of the country is for a Stray mother and her litter to be captured with the intention of finding homes for all. That mom gave birth at-large suggests that she is feral, meaning she's gone wild. It only takes a few generations for a feral dog's behavior to be identical to that of a truly wild canid. This wildness is passed down to her pups.

The first-generation feral dog is somewhat domesticatible and will probably do well with other dogs. If raised amongst humans from an early age, these pups will be fine. Where it gets dicey is with the more mature Imp who has learned to be leery of humans from his mom.

Around here, dogs are being trucked up from the south *en masse,* often with little to no information on their background or who belongs with whom. Guessing one's age and mix is a crapshoot. Cozy was listed as a ten-week-old German Shepherd/Lab-mix but I dubbed her a six-week-week-old Dachsweiler (Dachshund/Rottweiler) who, at four-months, morphed into a Beagleman (Beagle/Doberman). This is the case with mixes from any source, of course, I just mention it here as one more complicating factor.

> *Sidebar: For dogs of unknown lineage, DNA testing is all the rage these days. There are a number of test kits that range in reliability and cost. The pricier kits have more breeds in their database and are more accurate. Some people test out of curiosity, others for breed-specific disorders. The kits have gotten more reliable over the years. When they first came out, Harvey, who absolutely everyone agreed was a Chihuahua/dachshund-mix tested 100% Rottweiler.*

The Rehomed Dog

"Allergies" and "moving" are the "check is in the mail" of dumped dogs. We in rescue roll our eyes (loudly) upon hearing this. Though it's impossible to disprove one's allergy, I am quite sure they *do* take dogs in Duluth. Of course there are legitimate reasons to Rehome one's dog, and I have done so myself. But please don't assume that, though Imp isn't Good Enough for you, an adopter's eager to snatch up your barker, biter or runaway. And everyone's looking for that "farm upstate."

Imp's range of reactions to being Rehomed is as diverse as my brother's and mine were to moving fifteen times in sixteen years. I became outgoing and made friends with minimal effort. My brother turned introverted and suspicious. As easily as I made friends, I let them go. My brother hung on to his few friends for life. Our adaptive strategies served our individual circuitry.

Two of my own dogs fall at opposite ends of the attachment spectrum. Kiana was two when I adopted her and mine was her fourth home. She's now fifteen and we love one another but her aloofness has kept us from truly bonding. Hodge Podge had already been in two homes and two shelters when I adopted him at five-months. Six years later, his clinginess overwhelms me. Curiously, as needy as Hodge is, he's never manifested any separation anxiety. With him, out of sight is out of mind.

A Cautionary Word on Rescuing

I have lived and worked with Rescued dogs for forty-plus years and believe most who work in Rescue and adopt a Rescued dog do so with the best of intentions. There also exists a marginal fringe that seems more interested in the perceived *cachet* of adopting a Rescue or in the number of dogs placed than the sustainability of the placement. Here are two examples:

1. A young, dating couple, both of whom work long hours and live in a rental studio apartment in a high-rise, adopted a robust hound-mix through a splashy Adoptathon that resembled an overstocked Toyota dealership. Arlo was one of 20+ dogs trucked up from Arkansas. Never having been indoors, Arlo would now be left home alone for fourteen hours without a break and walked around the block three times daily. I was called in because Arlo trashed the apartment the first time home alone. At the current trajectory, Arlo's harming himself is certain. How the rescue group thought this was an appropriate placement is beyond me. I even question the motivation of "rescuing" these dogs to begin with.

   Arlo arrived in Connecticut in exquisite physical condition, displayed zero hand shyness or any signs of trauma and is a gentle, trusting soul. Apparently, the other "rescued" dogs are in comparable shape. The dogs were confiscated from a man outside Fayetteville who was eccentric but loved and took good care of the dogs in his own way. They weren't living in squalor; they were simply living outdoors, as dogs in the south often do. Like the do-gooders who seized those Haitian non-orphans, rescuing should be about what's best for the rescued not the rescuer.

2. A handsome couple flew home a stray puppy and her mother from a Caribbean vacation in the dead of winter and promptly notified the local news of their selflessness. It was far too cold for these tropical dogs to venture outdoors and they were far too freaked to be inside, so they withdrew to the far corner of the spare garage. This is where they stayed 24/7, relieving themselves in a litter box behind the BMW. In response to my suggesting that for less effort, money and wear-and-tear, the duo could have been spayed and released to sip daiquiris in the sun, the husband asked, "But where's the fun in that?"

P.S. I received an email six months after our session saying, "You'll be happy to know we separated the girls and each found a home." Happy? I was not.

Foster Care

With a glut of Rescue Groups popping up, many (most?) lack a brick and mortar facility and so they enlist a network of volunteers to Foster dogs awaiting a permanent home. This is a beautiful thing. Make that, *usually* beautiful. The benefits of being included in a loving home are clearly preferable to the alternatives. However, not all homes are all that loving.

Of late, two disturbing trends have emerged. The first involves dogs being shuttled between multiple Foster Homes, with some lasting a mere day or two. The problem is that no one told old Imp his new digs were only temporary. With each fleeting placement, Imp's confidence and, in turn, his long-term adoptability diminishes. One pup might develop debilitating separation anxiety while another shuts down and can't bond with anyone and a third neither bonds nor tolerates being alone. I often hear the original Foster Caretakers say that the now anxious Imp "wasn't like that here." And I believe them. However, "here" may have been multiple homes ago.

The second trend is to warehouse dogs interminably. Like an inmate who has been institutionalized too long, warehoused Imp may be unable to adjust to life beyond bars.

Again, these complications are of the Marginal Fringe's making. Believing that knowing better means doing better. I mention this to expand the conversation in hopes of reducing rescue recidivism.

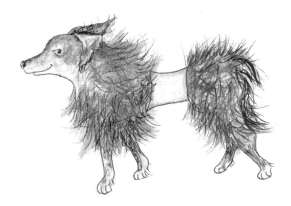

CHAPTER 9

Remedies For The Rescued Dog

Whether Imp was lovingly reared or brutally abused, whether he was feral or rehomed, it is rare for a Rescued Dog to arrive without baggage. For some super sensitive souls, simply adjusting to a new and improved home is unnerving.

Timidity

Timidity is common in dogs of questionable upbringing. Because fear is the main reason dogs bite, Timidity is a concern to take seriously. Timidity can be the result of nature or nurture, making the genetically Timid dog who was feral or mistreated a tinderbox of despair.

The primary mistake people make with a Timid dog (or person) is coming on too strongly too fast. This typically does more harm than good. Fear's potency was hammered home when I worked with monkeys in Sri Lanka and encountered scores of emaciated street dogs. Despite my best efforts to be ingratiating, these dogs refused to take food from my outstretched hand. Their fear of me trumped their hunger. One puppy I named Topo Gigio seemed unusually receptive. On day ten, Topo licked rice from my hand when another volunteer clapped. I never saw the pup again.

Suspicion is the feral dog's default response to novelty with the most mundane, a potential bogeyman. Cozy had been here three months when she freaked at the sight of kitchen tongs. She recovered more quickly than I imagine Topo Gigio would, but the initial reaction is the same.

After all of these years, I am thrilled when something useful occurs to me for the first time. This just happened. Long story short, a Havanese puppy who tends towards Timidity but is comfortable with the entire family and me is petrified of the husband, a total doll. While observing their interaction I found that, in meaning to be gentle, Gino acted tentative and a little nervous. This kept the pup on guard. Projecting confidence builds confidence. I am often asked how I get the results I do and I always answer, "Because I am confident I can."

Desensitization and Counterconditioning

Whatever Imp's upbringing, a systematic program of Desensitization and Counterconditioning is the heart and soul of overcoming fear. Desensitization means making Imp less sensitive to a stressor by demonstrating its irrelevance through progressively more intense exposure to it. Counterconditioning means teaching the opposite by offering Imp good things in the stressor's presence. Food is the best "good thing" and a superb icebreaker, so have liver bits, cheese or a Hebrew National handy.

We all have a personal space comfort zone that, when encroached upon, causes apprehension. Feral dogs are acutely aware of this boundary and have aced the flight feature of the fight, flight, freeze trilogy, so make sure the perimeters are secure.

Be seated when first meeting Imp and position yourself perpendicularly to him with food in a low-held hand. Keep all movements small and your voice soft. No eye contact. If he hangs back or does the approach/ avoidance dance, as long as there's no growling, casually toss food underhand as close as possible without spooking him. Imp's ignoring the food means he's not ready. No biggy, just leave it there and try again later.

Once Imp eats the tossed food, incrementally decrease the distance between the two of you by using today's demarcation as tomorrow's starting point. After he takes food out of your hand for a few consecutive days, begin layering in other fun stuff like a woods walk, Frisbee or shoe shopping. How fast to proceed is the wild card. Always err on the side of slow and expect regressions. Here, I typically split the difference by lowering my expectations slightly while still requiring Imp to meet me halfway. And I always end on a high.

Whistle While You Worry

By conveying calm confidence you set the tone for fearful Imp to respond in kind. If you catch yourself tensing, sing. No kidding, sing. A different part of the brain is engaged when we sing masking anxiety the spoken voice transmits. I suspect those happy hormones singing releases have a lot to do with it, too.

Did you know that people with severe stutters sing stammer-free? It's true. I've been telling clients this for years as many rolled their eyes thinking, I suspect, that was just me being all woo-woo. That's until the movie *The King's Speech* came out in 2010 and made an honest woman of me. I recently learned that Ed Sheeran also sang to overcome stuttering. Knowing this, when working with a biting dog or if trimming my parrots' nails, I break into show tunes. This technique is not recommended on a job interview or blind date.

P.S. Not being a whistler, I can't say whether whistling garners similar results. Still, if you're game, why not put your lips together and blow?

What If You Don't Know Anything About Imp's Past?

Unless yours was a private adoption, chances are you'll know little, if anything, about Imp's background, his age or even his elements. I appreciate how frustrating this can be, especially when a problem pops up. However, in all but the most severe cases, it isn't necessary to know the origin of a behavior to fix it.

Four months after adopting two-year-old Kiana from her third family, I swung my newspaper overhead to shoo away a bee. This caused Kiana to bolt through the screen door and flee to the furthest corner of the yard where she cowered beneath a bush and released her anal glands while trembling inconsolably. As you may know, many people think that swatting a dog with a rolled newspaper is acceptable because it's not especially painful. I disagree. The aggression behind the smack is what harms. With Kiana, it was easy to infer that this is how she'd been disciplined, making the desensitization/counterconditioning Rx obvious.

If your rehomed Imp either growls at or hides from someone of a different race or body type, it's tempting to assume prior abuse by individuals who looked similarly. What is equally likely, though, is that Imp never saw anyone who looked like that and the lack of familiarity is what scares him.

Whether Imp hides from an umbrella-toting bearded man or attacks the broom because he'd never seen one before or one hurt him intentionally or by accident, Desensitize him to the object of his fear while Counterconditioning him to feel better in its presence. With Kiana, I tossed treats to coincide with first lifting, then scrunching and ultimately swinging The New York Times until she learned its insignificance. And, awkward though it was, I arranged a Desensitization/ Counterconditioning set-up with an amputee from around the corner

whose path my dogs and I crossed daily. Carl was thrilled to bits when Buddha finally stopped snarling at him.

Separation Anxiety Disorder (SAD)

Separation Anxiety Disorder is the most serious problem impacting rehomed dogs and it's the most difficult to resolve as it exists exclusively in our absence. There are many misunderstandings about what constitutes Separation Anxiety, so let me first tell you what it is not.

All dogs dislike being alone. That Imp seems unhappy when you leave and thrilled when you return is perfectly normal. Many dogs without SAD follow their people from room to room and some with it don't. Following, per se, is therefore not diagnostic.

True Separation Anxiety is a phobic-like reaction to being alone that can manifest in one or more of the following ways: incessant whining, barking, howling, pacing, panting, drooling, extreme chewing, self-mutilation, incontinence, escaping, scratching and/or chewing at or around exit doors and windows. As with most phobias, the symptoms frequently take on a life of their own.

Many of the manifestations of Separation Anxiety are symptomatic of other issues. This causes some people to misinterpret what's wrong and react angrily upon returning home. Doing so exacerbates Imp's anxiety and, in turn, its expression. What's confusing is that dogs with Separation Anxiety tend to be exceptionally calm and relaxed in our presence making it impossible to imagine one so out of control when alone.

My thirteen-year-old Australian Shepherd-mix, Buddha, had been thrown out of a moving car on the Merritt Parkway at three-weeks. I adopted Buddha from a shelter soon thereafter when they'd decided to euthanize her, convinced that her inability to be left alone for even a few minutes would make her unadoptable. Buddha's anxiety was generalized, with being left, its primary trigger. She and I muddled through the first few months by my taking her on jobs or dropping her off with a friend and I cancelled all extra-curricular activities. As profound as Buddha's Separation Anxiety was, even at its peak, she seemed *blasé* about being with me. To this day, Bu is always within belly-rubbing reach yet acts as if she landed there by accident.

Separation Anxiety is also seen in dogs who were lost and then found by their family of origin and in those accustomed to someone always being around and then circumstances change. I am working with a beloved dog whose people both work from home. Lola accompanies them on errands and to the gym and is inconsolable on those rare occasions when alone. So don't do this.

Because SAD is such a big deal to fix, and because lifestyle unforeseens are unforeseeable,the following preventative measures make sense.

1. From the beginning, downplay your comings and goings and come and go often, if only to get the mail. As with a 747, arrivals and departures are problem spots. No matter how you feel about leaving or returning, act nonchalant—you're not the Messiah after all.

2. Dogs are naturally routinized; predictability is therefore important. Flexibility is equally important, so deliberately alter your routine from time to time. Missed trains and traffic jams happen.

3. Mondays, especially following holiday weekends, are tough on Imp. Though it's a bonus to have extra time together, please don't think that never being away from Imp over the weekend will compensate for all the hours you work.

4. Poop Imp out before leaving. A tired pup is less apt to be anxious. And make sure his biological needs are met.

5. If Imp is crated while home alone, play around with its placement. I've found that some dogs feel more secure when able to see the exit door and others, less so. Wherever the crate is situated, have comfy bedding inside that you've infused with your scent and a few safe toys. Many pups prefer the cool of the crate's floor in hot weather so use scrunchable bedding that Imp can shove aside. A clip-on water bottle or bowl is fine.

Before reading through the baby steps needed to reverse full-blown Separation Anxiety and having an anxiety attack yourself, please know that in severe cases a strictly behavioral approach is probably too slow and subtle. Here, I'd recommend temporarily augmenting the following program with one of the FDA approved prescription medications for Separation Anxiety. These tout a 70% success rate and are of the Prozac generation of drugs that will change Imp's brain chemistry without sedating him. The point is to massively re-condition Imp to tolerate alone time while under the drug's influence in hopes that, once weaned, his newfound self-confidence endures.

Please know that I'm no pill popper, and I consider it wimpy to take a Tylenol until my fever tops 102, but had these drugs existed in Mowgli or Buddha's day, you best believe I'd have used them. They typically take a few weeks to be fully effective, and you need a veterinarian's prescription after blood work, so I'd wait for Imp to reap the drug's full benefits to implement the following behavioral program whole hog.

In the meantime, try a natural supplement like Rescue Remedy and/ or a calming collar or plug-in diffuser. These are either infused with pheromones or herbal blends and take the edge off without side effects. In mild-to-moderate cases of Separation Anxiety, this may be all that's needed. Whether or not you use natural or chemical supplementation, all of the following is applicable.

Classic Desensitization and Counterconditioning is your ticket to resolving Separation Anxiety, so first identify the trigger that sets Imp's ungluing in motion. We all tend to do the same thing right before leaving the house like downing a donut, grabbing our keys or arming the alarm. Keys are a common stimulus, so let's go with them. Practice each of the following steps as its own event over a weekend or when you have no other agenda, and only advance from A to B once Imp is symptom-free. In acute cases, it could take weeks to complete the course even with drug support. Promise you won't rush.

Heads up! Any of the following steps could backfire and intensify a severely anxious Imp's symptoms. If so, discontinue and seek professional help.

a. Instead of hanging the keys on their usual hook by the backdoor, lay them on the end table next to the sofa where Imp and you spend quality time *schmoozing*. At random intervals, jiggle the keys while humming and then go back to your book. Better yet, keep reading while jiggling as further proof of the keys' insignificance. You should be able to breeze through this step.

b. Later, lift the keys and sashay over to the exit door all loosey-goosey, hang the keys on the hook and go back to your cozy spot—end of discussion. Unless this stresses Imp, no need to repeat. That's is enough for today.

c. Jiggle those wretched keys at the door while unemotionally handing Imp a scrumptious treat or his best toy. Offer the loot before Imp acts out to avoid reinforcing his angst. Now return the keys to the hook and mosey back to the sofa. This step will probably need a number of repetitions.

d. Assuming Imp tolerated the key tickling; it's time to leave but not actually go anywhere. Before calmly leaving, hand Imp the treat and/or toy. If the toy squeaks, squeak it; if it has a cavity that can be fill with snacks, stuff it as described on page 93 under chewing. Close the door and calmly return before Imp has time to panic. Remember to greet him unemotionally and amble back to the couch. From here, come and go repeatedly to demonstrate what a nothing event this is while gradually elongating the away time to twenty minutes. Though I couldn't tell you why, twenty minutes is a magical timeframe for many dogs.

e. Now the moment of reckoning—deep breath—time to actually leave. After exiting, get in the car or push the elevator button, drive around the block or hang in the lobby for a few minutes, return and coolly ask, "How you doin'?" Now change the subject by moving on to what would naturally happen next: check the mail, change out of your works clothes, pee - whatever. From here, repeat and extend away time while maintaining meaningful markers like mealtime and trips to the park. With enough comings and goings, Imp will ultimately hit critical mass and smack himself upside the head wondering what all the *hoopla* had been about.

LET ME TELL YOU ABOUT MR. AND MRS. MAYER'S DOG, OSCAR, a sensitive Pit Bull adopted through rescue. Mrs. Mayer described Oscar as the gentlest, calmest, sweetest dog in the whole wide world but for his "pesky barking" when home alone in their condo. A neighbor clocked his barking at three hours. Like being a model citizen but for the burglaries, Oscar's "pesky" problem made him *persona non grata* in the retirement community.

Fearing eviction, the Mayers took Oscar in the car with them where he silently accepted alone time. This is quite common for dogs with Separation Anxiety. Once it turned too hot for Oscar to be left in the car, at a fellow professional's recommendation, the Mayers bought an electric shock collar that zapped the poor dog every time he opened his mouth when home alone in the condo. This caused Oscar to shoot liquid diarrhea and he soon generalized his anxiety to the car, precluding that option no matter the weather.

As dire as this sounds, with medication and a rigorous behavior modification program like the one discussed, Oscar was weaned off the meds after six-months and has remained symptom free for two years.

OLIVER'S STORY: A UNIQUE CASE OF SEPARATION ANXIETY

Greg adopted 205 pound Oliver, an English Mastiff, when his first family could no longer afford to care for him. Oliver adapted without incident and bonded instantly with Speed, the resident Greyhound. Speed died unexpectedly thirteen months later. The first time Greg returned home thereafter, the contents of his modest home were mostly destroyed. We're talking a sectional sofa, two overstuffed chairs, countless books, three doors, Venetian Blinds and more. It wasn't clear what caused the deep gash on Oliver's side, but blood splatter freckled the ceiling.

Overwhelming though this seemed at first, after two weeks on meds, we were able to systematically condition Oliver to tolerate being alone. Like Oscar, Oliver was weaned off meds in six months and now accepts being home alone with a walker coming midday.

Crate Anxiety vs. Separation Anxiety

Some pups who panic in a crate handle freedom surprisingly well. As many are only crated when home alone, it's easy to confuse Crate Anxiety with Separation Anxiety. This distinction is only discovered once Imp is no longer crated.

Since hearing of one desperate dog who died from injuries incurred while attempting to bust out of his crate, I've advised clients whose dogs panic to discontinue using a crate and find another means of containing Imp. However, many were afraid to try for fear Imp would trash the house and gave him away instead. As I'd never actually lived with a pup

with Crate Anxiety and hadn't proofed alternative containment options, it was a difficult concept to sell to wary adopters.

Then I adopted Doc, my scrumptious Australian Shepherd-mix who was trucked up from Tennessee. On Doc's third day here I crated him for fifteen minutes to test-drive his tolerance and returned to find him at the door covered in cuts. Doc had busted out of a locked, all metal crate. This poor, sweet little boy was as inconsolable as any puppy I've ever seen.

Now that I've successfully practiced with Doc what I long preached, I am now able to present a more compelling argument to try the following crate-free option with home alone Imp. The same preparatory measures for Separation Anxiety are also applicable to Crate Anxiety.

Thinking Outside The Box: Safely Containing Anxious Imp *Sans* Crate

Select a small, cozy space where Imp has or can be fed and adorn it with toys, treats, a plug-in Calming Diffuser, WiFi and comfortable bedding that smells like you. A centrally located bathroom or mudroom will do.

Use a gate across the main or only doorway to contain well-exercised Imp in his *de facto* den. For whatever reason, dogs who panic behind a closed door usually relax if they can see out. Being claustrophobic myself, I can relate. With a jumper, double-decker one gate atop another. Spray non-removable objects like molding or cabinets with a Chewing Aversive and place a dog-safe bone nearby. Hand Imp his fav toy when saying *adieu*, come and go calmly while incrementally elongating away time.

Once Imp accepts this arrangement without argument for at least five consecutive days, gradually expand his domain by closing ancillary doors and/or using gates so that in six-weeks he seamlessly segues into his modified turf.

This is exactly what I did with Doc who, other than filleting *The Joy of Cooking*, has accepted this arrangement without incident to this day.

Odds and Ends

1. As it could make or break Imp's recovery, I want to be sure you understand why dispassionate comings and goings are essential. Remember, Imp is incapable of understanding that you're upset *for* him, he's certain it's *at* him, so a dramatic goodbye communicates, "You're right, Imp, my leaving sucks." Conversely, returning home a wreck over how he might have fared could make him fear seeing you. At the very least, it squelches the highlight of his day. An overly adoring reunion also runs the risk of amplifying Imp's loneliness by comparison.

2. Dogs don't bond with each family member equally so, while it's wonderful to get everyone in on the act, Imp's main person needs to do the brunt of the work. For this program to be a true test, Imp must be left without any humans home, though other critters are fine. And to avoid an Oliver-like meltdown, in homes with multiple dogs, occasionally rehearse Imp's being home all alone preemptively.

3. You may have been told that leaving the TV or radio on is comforting. I agree that if the TV or radio is on a lot when you're home, it's an extension of your being there and is a good idea. If, however, you only turn the stereo on upon leaving, it signals your departure and could either spark or amplify Imp's anxiety.

4. Tempting though it is to say, "stay" upon leaving, don't. Stay is a time-limited request and requires a release. Also, to say, "stay" while Imp's despondent about being abandoned compromises its life-saving effectiveness if needed to prevent his darting across a road. Here, a casual "toot-a-loo" will do.

5. Running a Nanny Cam while Imp's home alone might identify a modifiable trigger.

6. Adoptive parents often feel hurt by Imp's Separation Anxiety believing that he should feel more secure, not less, now that he's got you. Here's how I understand it: Let's say you used to live in a windowless basement apartment by the boiler with orange

crates for end tables and a mattress on the floor, and now you're in a McMansion on thirteen acres. You never bothered to lock the apartment's doors but you're now a wreck over the security guard's drinking. So it is with Imp's upgrade.

7. Even if Imp seems disinterested in the toy you hand him before leaving, do so anyway. Being the last thing you handled, its fragrant presence reminds Imp of you and tells him to seek that out if in need of a chew.

I concocted a little experiment with my puppy Stinky who, while being weaned from his crate, always greeted me at the door holding something of mine in his mouth: a shoe, book or even my hairbrush. The item was gooey but never damaged. Then I realized I had changed out of those shoes or brushed my hair right before leaving the house. So I bought seven identical fuzzy balls with a squeaker - Stinky's favorites - and wrote M on Monday's, a T on Tuesday's, etc. I bunched all seven by the exit door and, before leaving Wednesday, I handed Stinky the W toy, and so forth. Guess who greeted me with the TH toy on Thursdays and the F on Fridays.

Finally, as satisfying as it is to rehabilitate a severely anxious Rescued Dog, it's a painstaking process that can easily overwhelm even we diehards. If this prospect makes you queasy, please pass. The last thing poor Imp needs is to be rehomed by you. And if you have your own separation issues, please work through them on your own time.

CHAPTER 10

It's Urine Not Uranium

Housebreaking is simply a matter location, location, location—that's it. We're not teaching Imp *what* to do but *where*. I shudder to think of all those normal puppies who are destroyed—emotionally and literally—due to geography. This is a quality of life priority, I know, but obsessing over Housebreaking at the expense of more substantive matters is as misplaced as obsessing over toilet training Junior while ignoring his pronounced speech impediment. When Imp goes off to Brandeis, sentimentality over his first well-placed poop is long forgotten. All healthy dogs, no matter the breed or size, can be Housebroken.

And there's a lot of lying about Housebreaking going on, almost a collective amnesia. Accomplished adults are made to feel inept because a neighbor, boss or in-law insists that her dog was 100% Housebroken and doing logarithms in a week. I frequently work with a family's second or third generation pup and witness upstanding citizens who look me squarely in the eyes and swear, "Wally never had an accident (or chewed the furniture or jumped on company or…)" and I clearly remember Wally as doing all of the above and then some.

The Ins & Outs of Housebreaking
Before Three Months

Baby puppies pee often and everywhere with a nearly nonexistent lag time between sensation and release. Your goal now is to whisk Imp outside upon awaking, greeting, playing or laughing and praise him for a job well done. I haven't found that treats hasten Housebreaking, so save them for where they're needed. When home alone or if unsupervisable, tuck Imp into a cozy crate that's situated where he'll feel the love. Multiple crates—one upstairs and another down—are fine. You will miss many a tinkle, we all do, just clean it up with a commercial odor neutralizer or white vinegar and move on. Three to four poops a day is natural at this age, so if Imp consistently goes more than that, you're probably feeding him too much. For now, just flush ill-placed poops.

Sidebar: I'm not big on limiting water. dogs only drink as much as they need. Restriction might make for less urine but it does so at the expense of Imp's health. Besides, some pups go into camel-mode and tank-up when water is sparse. Good thing I trusted my gut when DJ was a baby as all he did was drink and pee, drink and pee. Had I listened to the first two vets who told me to restrict his water he'd have died in days. DJ was diagnosed with diabetes insipidus, admittedly an extremely rare disease, but I'm just saying...

Between Three and Four Months

In addition to bringing Imp outside presumptively, it's time to teach him to ask. A to-die-for trick that I should have mentioned earlier is the **Bell on The Door**. From the handle of the exit door(s), hang a bell that's low enough for Imp to nose or paw without jumping. Every time you take him outside, jingle the bell while saying something like, "So you wanna go out, or what?" With enough, "So you...or whats?" clever Imp will catch on that the bell ringing makes the door open and tinkle it himself. Could you die?

Sidebar: I am often asked how to teach Imp to bark when asking to go out and I always answer, "You don't." By rewarding barking, you run the risk of creating a bossy barker, which is way harder to undo than Housebreaking is to do. Bossy Barking will be addressed on page 102 in "Nuisance Barking."

Now that you understand a dog's sense of timing, you see why it's essential to catch Imp in the act for him to understand it's the peeing or pooping indoors that's unacceptable, not the act itself. Because puppies often meander out of sight to wiz, rather than follow Imp about, use gates and closed doors to keep him in sight. Aside from being incredibly annoying, following Imp suggests that he's in charge and you are the subordinate. The top dog always leads.

Prevention, of course, is better than intervention, so observe Imp's body language right before he squats. Does he circle, whine, sniff in a specific way, kink his tail or reach for a smoke? Once the behavior's recognized, sashay signaling Imp to the door, ring the bell and take him out. If he's as brilliant as my Cozy, he'll catch on in a matter of days. Occasionally, a pup is scared of the bell, doesn't get it or he rings it all the ding-dong day. Not to worry, discontinue using the bell and rely on observation to tell you it's time.

And in case you haven't already taught Imp a code word to relieve himself, it's not too late. While Imp's in the act, drone, "Get busy, Hurry up, Donald Trump..." whatever. With enough repetition, whether you're in the midst of nor'easter or on I-95, Donald Trump will inspire a dump.

Sidebar: I hate to insult you by sharing something so absurd, but the following comes up more often than you might think. I was just with a woman who spent the first twenty minutes of our 90-minute session yelling at the 11-week-old Labrador to, "Go potty!" on a precise patch of lawn when

all Jake wanted to do was a dig a hole, something Ma yelled at him not to do. In response to my saying for the fourth time, "perhaps Jake doesn't need to relieve himself now," Ma snapped, "I read online that he should make when and where I tell him." I then explained (with an edge) that there has to be something in there to come out. Ma feigned understanding this, though I was not convinced.

What to do if you observe Imp having an accident? Actually, a well-caught mistake followed by a prompt redirect is worth its weight. Correct and Redirect is your training mantra. Without rancor or discourse say, "No!" mid-squat, escort Imp over to the door, jiggle the bell to communicate, *you coulda asked*, pick up the poop with a paper towel and take it outside with Imp to deposit where it belongs. Translocating sopped-up urine is too subtle to bother, but still take Imp out. To Correct without a Redirect is half a thought—a missed opportunity. But don't go overboard with the correction lest Imp thinks he shouldn't go in front of you and so he waits until you turn your back to unload behind potted palm.

Four to Six Months

If Imp is 80% housebroken at four months he'll easily be 100% by six. Every accident is a double negative - and not the good kind - in that you've missed an opportunity to reinforce a job well done and you still have to clean up a mess.

The Book on Paper Training

There are some people who, due to health, climate or lethargy, choose to permanently Paper Train their dog. If this is okay with you, it's okay with me. Moving forward, Paper Trainers substitute Paper for outside and it'll fly.

For the rest of us, rather than actively Paper Training infant Imp, a passive approach frees you up and is perfectly acceptable. The point of passive Paper Training is to localize the indoor toilet until Imp masters the outdoors. I'd recommend placing the paper on a spot he's cottoned to, ideally close to the exit door, with the intention of ultimately inching it outside.

There are all sorts of pricey plastic-lined pads that protect the floor and are tidier than newspaper. Some pads are even infused with a uriney-scent making one wonder, who thinks up this stuff, anyway? The problem with pads is that many pups drag them around and/or shred them to bits making a mess that's more work to clean up than taking Imp out would have been. Most pups prefer to pee on something absorbent, so pick up throw rugs making the paper/pad the most absorbent option. And if you'd prefer to use a litter box to paper, be my guest.

Marking and Submissive Urination

Neither Marking nor Submissive Urination has anything to do with Housebreaking but, while we're in urine, here goes.

Marking is when Imp squirts urine on a targeted object to say, "Mine!" before swaggering off to high-five his homies. Marking is a visceral reaction to a potent stimulus, usually a scent. Intact males are most apt to Mark with leg lifted, but even a gender-conflicted spayed female might wait in line to leave her pheromone-steeped calling card.

While it's natural for Imp to Mark up the woods, the committed Marker might bring his handiwork indoors. This is frowned upon in Connecticut. The addition of a new puppy, menstruation, a soggy diaper or urine tracked in on one's shoes might elicit a spritz. Marking can also be an expression of displaced frustration to a woodchuck just beyond the picture window or a stuck car alarm.

Because Marking is involuntary, attempts to correct it are as futile as punishing a sneeze. The good news is that, with a novice Marker, neutering will eliminate the urge altogether and is 80% successful even with master Markers. Be patient, it could take many weeks for neutering's benefits to kick in.

Imp's Marking during a walk around the block is usually fine—he needs a life, after all—but for the territorially aggressive dog or the runaway, Marking expands Imp's home turf compelling frequent revisiting updates. The easiest way to prevent Marking on a quiet suburban or country road is to walk in the middle of the street where there are fewer aromas and no vertical surfaces, the preferred spritzee. Otherwise, jogging could override Imp's need to Mark until the neutering takes hold.

Submissive Urination is an unconscious action that communicates the sensitive urinator's lowly status while saying, "I respect you and mean no harm." Submission Urination can be of the Excitement or Fear-based persuasion.

Excitement Urination is primarily a puppy event, girls more than boys. I consider it a bad day if I don't get piddled on at least once. Speaking of piddle, that was my dog, Plain Jane's, moniker. As with all excitement urinators, PJ didn't even know she was tinkling, so we simply downplayed greetings and said, "Hey" outside until Piddle sobered up at a year.

Fear-based Urination is a symptom of low self-esteem that must be ignored while Imp's confidence is bolstered elsewhere.

De-Crating Imp

Some of you may choose to keep Imp crated when home alone and/ or overnight for life. For the rest of us who want to get rid of the ugly old thing once Imp's housebroken and no longer chewing our stuff, here's what to do.

I learned the hard way decades ago with Monty, my Dobuki (Doberman/Saluki-mix), not to dispense with a Crate altogether before ten months as there's frequently a chewing regression then. Still, here's how to begin weaning home alone Imp's reliance on the Crate between eight and ten months. These timeframes, like all timeframes, are not set in stone.

Get well-exercised Imp into the Crate as usual, hand him that special toy and close the Crate door partially, like you simply forgot to shut it all the way. Now leave the house nonchalantly. Return after a minute or two and, whether Imp meets you at the door or stays in the Crate, proceed calmly with what would normally happen next. Incrementally expand Imp's home alone time with the door ajar so that by ten months to one year, assuming he has proven reliable thus far, forego the door-closing charade and simply hand Imp that toy upon leaving the house in earnest.

Remember, it's perfectly fine to keep certain rooms off limits. While actively De-Crating Imp, continued to close the crate door for real when you leave the house for a hunk of time. And in case you're wondering about the Crate door-closing ruse, some sensitive souls stay in it as if they didn't even notice it wasn't locked while building their cage-free confidence. This was the case with Cozy. I spared her the embarrassment of pointing that out.

Finally, whether or not you plan on using the Crate permanently, if you have the room, keep one set up to occasionally toss Imp into to minimize future angst should he need containment due to injury or when malodorous.

Debunking Common Housebreaking Myths

1. Once a puppy goes in the house you'll never get rid of the odor. This is just plain stupid thinking, yet I hear it all the time. While we're on stupid, what's with the euphemisms adults use when talking about housebreaking? A judge referred to her Lhasa Apso's "# 2s," a truck driver called them, "Tootsie Rolls," and an opera singer, "Tee-tees."

2. A puppy will never have an accident in his crate. True, it is natural for dogs to leave their sleeping quarters to relieve themselves but, if confined too long or if sick, they're going to go. I might under similar circumstances, myself. Pups raised in squalor at unsavory pet shops or over-crowded shelters may have lost the desire to stay clean. If baby Imp makes wherever he sleeps, I'd contain him in a large enough area so he won't wallow in it. While we're on crate size, I think too many people go overboard minimizing floor space. It is true that containing a teacup Shit Tzu is a palatial crate defeats its purpose. It is also true that stuffing an Irish Wolfhound into one without room to stand upright or stretch is cruel.

3. Push Imp's nose in his mess. Are you kidding me? Dogs adore the scent of pee and poop. And if you were positive the nose shove worked with your last pup, trust me, your ire was all that was punitive. Imp got housebroken despite, not because of it.

4. Once you start using paper you're stuck with it forever. Like diapers, all babies can be weaned in time.

5. Though not technically a myth, stop fretting over poop: it's the pee that'll come back to bite you in the butt. Speaking of which, a nifty CSI-style way to locate stale pee is with a handheld Black Light.

Chapter 11

Educating Imp
No Frills Basic Training

ormal Obedience Training is full of ornamental embellishments like the Finish where Imp circles his "Master" precisely as part of heel. These flourishes will not be taught here. Before diving in, a little background...

When I started doing this work in 1980, it was believed that dogs were simply bundles of conditioned responses, devoid of emotions, who lived simply to please us. Not buying this, I was considered a heretic.

Nowadays, the prevailing never-say-no tide goes overboard the other way, but at least it's in the too rich/too thin direction. Whatever your orientation, the laws governing dog behavior are the same as for the rest of us: behaviors endure with reinforcement—positive or negative—and extinguish without it. Whether you're housebreaking the puppy, toilet training your toddler or teaching your *fiancé* to put the toilet seat down, the goal is to identify what motivates desirable behaviors and use these incentives to your advantage. Where I split from the hardcore behavioral camp is that I also recognize and revere dogs' rich emotional range. Incorporating this awareness into a training program is the difference between technique and artistry. Here, then, is what every Imp needs to know.

Look At Me

Look at Me is a nifty little pre-training exercise. Like stretching, Look at Me is no great shakes on its own, but as the warm-up to a marathon, you're primed for success. Eye contact between Imp and you can be as connecting or as intimidating as between you and your Mom. Our goal is to communicate, not bully, so keep your eyes soft while tweaking your fingers in front of Imp's eyes and then flitter them up to your own eyes and softly say, "Look at me." When Cozy has a hard time composing herself, Look at Me brings her focus back to me so I can direct her to Sit or Stay or Go Lie Down.

Sit Happens

Sit is the Baking Soda of dog training. Brush your teeth with Sit, deodorize the 'fridge with Sit, freshen the litter box with it. When in doubt, all-purpose Sit is the way to go.

Think of your asking Imp to Sit as meaning, *I'm in control*, and Imp's doing so as his saying, *please*, so sprinkle Sit throughout the day. Sit makes the door open. Sit makes food happen. Balls get thrown following Sit.

Here's How To Teach Sit

Face or stand next to Imp and in a soft natural voice say, "Imp, Sit," while scooping your cupped hand up and over his head starting at chest level and arching back towards his butt. Stand close and only lift your hand a few inches above his head, no touching. Tweak or snap your fingers to engage Imp's eyes and, as his head moves up and back to follow your hand, his rear goes down. *Voila*, Sit Happens.

This is a good time to talk about Positive Reinforcement, which immediately follows the desirable behavior. There are three forms of

Positive Reinforcement: verbal, manual and material, with food being the preferred canine currency. But please don't underestimate the benefits of touch and singsongy praise. Think of petting and accolades as Imp's baseline salary with treats being a frequent bonus.

After Imp Sits, praise him while petting his chest and offering a treat. I know, it's like rubbing your belly while patting your head, but give it a go. You're luring Imp to Sit with your naked hand not the treat, so keep food in a pocket or pouch until needed lest he accost your treat-toting hand.

With three forms of reinforcement to choose from, mix it up. Offer treats regularly at first and then randomize them in frequency and desirability to keep Imp on his toes. (This will be discussed further with Come When Called.) A treat should be special, not his boring old kibble or a Cheerio, though small is fine—Imp doesn't care about size. This is the fundamental difference between dogs and men.

Sidebar: Never force Imp into position by pushing down his rear for Sit or yanking out his legs for Down. Coercion creates resistance and teaches Imp to tolerate your positioning him rather than doing it himself. Our goal is to motivate Imp to offer the behavior freely—to own it.

If Sit Doesn't Happen

1. Check that you're not standing too far away. You want to be cross-eyed close.

2. Make sure your signaling hand is only a few inches over Imp's head. Too high will encourage jumping.

3. Imp may need traction. Work on grass or a rug.

4. Sitting is painful if Imp has bad hips or knees. Go straight to Lie Down and have your vet check poor Imp out.

5. If all else fails, a Coercion-Lite trick is to reach under Imp's head and hold on to the bottom of the collar while lifting up and a bit back. Though I can't tell you why, Imp's butt should go down. Of course, label his Sitting so you can quick phase out the Collar Lift and have the behavior endure.

Leave It and Drop It

My Hodge Podge was slated to be killed at five-months by his prior owner because he ferociously guarded a tissue. That's right, a tissue.

Object guarding, especially in strays and those who have been deprived, often assumes irrational proportions with a discarded butter wrapper being indistinguishable from prime ribs.

Leave It means *don't pick the thing up to begin with*, and Drop It means *let me have what you (shouldn't have) picked up*. Both "its" could save Imp's life.

Leave It

The Setup: Select a few legal and illegal objects and, in case the setup backfires, make sure the contraband is harmless. For the illicit, I'm going with a paper napkin, a flip-flop and a vitamin C capsule. For what's acceptable, a quacking duck, string cheese and a Kong toy.

Drop your scrunched napkin on the floor and allow Imp to sniff it. Should he attempt to pick the napkin up, calmly say, "Leave It" and if you get lucky, Imp will. Now say, "Sit" and toss the duck while saying something generic like, "Get your baby." If hearing Leave It isn't enough, step on the napkin to prevent Imp's absconding with it and then redirect.

Another way to set Imp up is to nonchalantly drop the napkin that's been pre-sprayed with the Chewing Aversive and time your Leave It to coordinate with his getting a mouthful.

If all else fails, tie a string around the contraband and, when Imp ignores your "Leave It", whisk the item away. But beware, many an Imp finds a soaring sandal hysterical and is even more attracted to it than one that lays limp.

Drop It

Drop It can either mean *put down what's in your mouth* or *let me take it without argument*. The difference being that, while it's easy for Imp to drop a remote control or slipper, lacking spitting muscles or a scooping first finger, a pill is too puny to spew, hence the taking without argument application. Think of Drop It as a trade; if you let go of that I'll give you this, with "this" being something of equal or greater value. And for the fetcher, Drop It means I'll toss your Frisbee again. And again. And again. And again…

To teach Imp to Drop something small, grip a little, hard treat between thumb and first finger. Offer Imp the treat and, as he clamps down, calmly say, "Drop It," then pull the treat away. He needs to understand that your fingers are allowed in his mouth, so they are a part of the setup. Repeat a few times then say, "Sit" to remind Imp you're still in control, and now release the treat while saying, "Okay" or "Take It." Next, try the same setup but instead of giving Imp that treat, offer something even better. Every now and again ask him to Drop It just for free as it's unlikely you'll always have snacks.

Now that we've taught Imp that Drop It is worth his while and we've made recovering bite-sized bits possible, it's time to supersize. Offer Imp a Nike, say, "Drop It" and upgrade to an Adidas. Just kidding, make it a Reebok. If he clamps down, grab hold of the protruding part and twist smartly while saying, "Drop It. Good boy, Sit." Now offer the replacement of equal or greater value.

In case you're worried that these automatic upgrades teach Imp to steal, I applaud your thoughtfulness and remind you of the importance of inserting the Sit in between Drop and the re-direct. Here, you're rewarding Imp's Sitting.

> *Sidebar: The secret to Leave It and Drop It working in real life is to maintain the same lightheartedness as in rehearsal. Panicking could cause Imp to flee in fear or to swallow the object, as if the intensity of your interest elevated its appeal. And in case you're worried that Imp'll clamp down on your fingers while offering bite-sized treats, having done this tons of times, I've never been hurt. Wearing gloves is fine, though, if you're worried.*

How Rehearsing Drop It Might Have Saved Baby Cozy's Life

I began teaching Cozy to Drop It almost immediately upon bringing her home at seven weeks. On her fourth day here, I heard what sounded like something metal that was completely contained within her mouth. I quick grabbed a treat, calmly asked her to Sit then said, "Drop It" and playfully pulled a thumbtack out of her puppy mouth.

Stay

I'm a stickler for Stay, which means *don't move from the spot until I release you.* Stay at the door when the pizza's delivered. Stay in the car until I grab hold of your leash to enter the Dog Park. And, God forbid Imp darts across the road, Stay there until I come get you. The difference between Staying on the curb or in the street is inches, hence my stringency. However, as long as Imp maintains his footprint, if asked to Sit Stay and he chooses to Lie Down and Stay, take it. This means Imp's settling in for the long haul. Besides, the Down Stay is typically more difficult to teach, so if Imp offers $20 when you only asked for $10, I wouldn't complain.

Here's How To Teach Stay

Once Imp's Sit is reliable, in your natural voice calmly say, "Good Boy, Stay," like it's one word. Sit-Good-Boy-Stay. The Stay hand signal is the universal one for STOP used by traffic cops and Diana Ross' Supremes, palms facing Imp, fingers pointing up. Your voice should be static, almost onomatopoetic. Say and signal Stay concurrently while you stand still, 2.3. Now pet Imp's chest on Good Boy and offer a treat taken from pocket or pouch. The treat marks the end of the sequence and the 2,3, is to help with your timing.

Stay is a progressive exercise, so incrementally expand the distance and duration. Stay for ten seconds from five feet, then thirty seconds from ten feet, etc. Upon returning to end Stay, occasionally lift little Imp or grab hold of big Imp's collar from below to demonstrate this as a possible outcome in an emergency.

Next, add distractions. Crinkle a potato chip bag, drop a crumpled paper towel or kick off an Ugg. If Imp stands, snap, No! and then step back to where he should have Stayed and start all over, nicely. Imp, Sit. Good boy, Stay. And so it goes.

Stay will soon be implicit in Sit. I don't ask my adult dogs to Sit and Stay, I simply say, "Sit" and they understand they're meant to Stay Sitting until released. I still break it down with Cozy, like teaching arm and leg movements separately before unifying them into the breaststroke.

In addition to returning to Imp, Stay can be ended by calling him to come. Stay is to come what addition is to subtraction—both essential but functionally opposite. I therefore prefer to have a solid Stay for at least five days before actively working on come so that each is understand as its own event.

Stay's Sticking Points

1. Less is more with Stay. Calmly say and signal, Stay just once while standing still. People tend to get frenetic and repeat Stay! Stay! Stay!... This communicates a lack of confidence on your part, an expectation Imp may well meet. By under doing it, Imp is required to concentrate; much like a Montessori teacher's speaking softly to hold her students' attention.

2. Make sure that you reach below not above his head upon returning. Over could be perceived as a dominance challenge and cause Imp to wince or take off.

3. Stand still while saying, "Stay." To be on the move blurs where Imp is meant to be. Take your time stepping away and in lengthening his Staying power.

4. Maintain the Stay hand signal throughout at first, and then thin out its usage over time. However, always signal Stay upon requesting it.

5. Stand upright. You want to be big with Stay and, as you'll soon see, small with its opposite, come when called.

6. This isn't specific to Stay but here is as a good a place as any to mention the importance of checking your voice tone when Correcting and Redirecting. Corrections should be a single stern, bark-like, "No!" followed by a calm, neutral redirect. Quickly switching from one tone to the other is key.

7. The importance of keeping the treat out of sight is especially important with Stay as it's a lure which works well with come, but is too tempting here.

8. A small but important detail is simply saying, "Stay," without mentioning Imp by name. Why? Most of us call, "Imp" when we mean to say, "come" so he might associate his name with motion. Stay is the absence of movement so, Imp, Stay sounds like move/don't move. *Capice?*

A Word on Hand Signals

I adore them, especially with Stay. By cultivating Imp's visual as well as verbal attentiveness, Hand Signals provide a second mode of communication, like learning French and Spanish. The most connected dogs I know are those taught Hand Signals. Another benefit is that elderly dogs may lose hearing before sight so, if conditioned to Hand Signals from early on, they'll look to you for guidance thereby easing the disorientation of old age.

Come When Called

Come When Called is the ultimate test of your ability to think like a dog and is a reflection of your relationship with Imp. Come is 20% technique, 80% psychology. Imp needs to feel safe to choose to Come to you. "Choose" is the operative word as Imp could choose not to.

People frequently assume Imp arrives factory-loaded knowing what Come means, so they call and call at the back door to no avail. Really stupid people then label him stubborn or defiant. Job #1 is to teach Imp what Come actually means.

The Passive Approach

As the carefree baby puppy tools your way, kneel, smile and spread your welcoming arms apart while happily saying, "Imp, Come." Now lavish incoming Imp with praise and offer a primo treat before releasing him to return to what he'd been doing. Call Imp at mealtime while lifting his jangly bowl. Call him to Come out of his crate and in anticipation of a fun walk. How cool is Come?

Think of Coming When Called as Imp's job, a job for which payment (food) is required. But Imp also needs to learn the value of volunteerism, so occasionally have him Come for free. This is called Intermittent Reinforcement. If Imp were to get paid for 100% of his Comes and you forget to bring treats to the beach, this would be viewed as a breach of contract thereby nullifying Imp's obligation to Come in the future.

Nana Daisy

In my group classes I tell the story of how, as a child, I visited my Nana Daisy every Sunday and she always had some little knick-knack for me. Every Sunday a knick-knack. One Sunday Daisy didn't make it to the toy store on account of her rheumatism. Bereft, and certain Daisy no longer loved me, I refused to ever visit her again. Had my Nana simply randomized the friggin' *tchotchkes* she and I would be sipping cocoa even as we speak.

Okay, that never actually happened, but it might have.

A Word on Randomization

We humans stink at this. I can't tell you how often I'm asked something like, "Is every other random enough?" Random's not relative, it's "unsystematic and without a predictable pattern." Even the simplest Imp can predict boy/girl, boy/girl.

Clickers

To spice up Come, let's add a Clicker. In case you don't already know, Clickers are little plastic boxes that, when compressed, make a distinctive chirping sound like the crickets we played with as kids.

First, teach Imp that the Click is a good sound by Clicking and then giving him a small treat. The Click is intended to travel and can be jarring if too close to Imp's ear. For this piece, muffle the Click in a pocket or behind your back. Click then treat. Repeat a few times and start walking around the house or yard Click then treating, Click then treating. Once Imp realizes the Click means a treat is imminent, put it all together by Clicking while knelt and, with a smile on your face and song in your heart call, Imp, Come! Now break out the bubbly as Imp busts a gut to get to you.

Wonder why we're adding a complicating element like the Clicker? Good question. There's a distinct crispness to the Click that cuts through a lot of ambient noise like wind, water and traffic while carrying over hill and dale without disturbing the neighbors. It's lightweight, inexpensive and, most importantly, everyone in the family can Click equally. Trust me, the results are usually dramatic.

Common Come Complications

Okay, now that the technical stuff's out of the way, the hard part is making Come work where the deer and antelope play. Remember my *spiel* about dogs being non-sequential learners and the importance of immediate reinforcement? If not, here's a quick recap as this is the crux of Come. The last thing Imp does is what he thinks you're acknowledging. So, even if he Comes When Called toting a decomposed skunk after a dip in the swamp before darting across the Interstate, he's a good boy. See the challenge? Responding angrily makes Imp reconsider returning the next time the swamp beckons.

To ensure you don't inadvertently teach Imp not to Come When Called, let's explore three serious, albeit common, pitfalls.

1. You leave infant Imp in the kitchen while you shower and return to discover he'd trashed the garbage. Annoyed, you call Imp over, he naïvely Comes and then you read him the riot act. WRONG! Imp's misdeed happened at 7:15, it's now 7:40 and the last thing he did was Come. This is pretty obvious. The next examples are more subtle.

2. Imp's out frolicking in the yard or free in the house and it's time to crate him because you've got a hair appointment. Wanting Imp to be as empty and exhausted as possible, you wait until the last second to call him in before dashing out the door. WRONG! Here, Come precedes abandonment.

3. You're at the off-leash Dog Park and Imp's partying with his peeps so you hold off calling him until it's time to go home. WRONG! Come means the end of fun.

Here's How to Handle These Three Scenarios

1. Leaving Imp unsupervised in the kitchen was your bad. Just clean up the mess and move on.

2. If you need to leave the house at 8:15, call Imp in at 8:00. A fifteen-minute buffer before heading out provides a safe disconnect from Coming.

3. Let's say you have an hour to spend at the Dog Park, call Imp ten times, offer eight treats, nine times release him to play-on and only one time Come means it's time to go. These are Good Enough odds for any Imp to take.

Don't worry; you won't have to be this deliberate forever. Remember learning to drive and spending forever getting the rearview mirror just right? So it is with calling Imp to Come.

Before you test Imp completely untethered in the park, use a safety net by tying a lightweight 20-foot rope to Imp's non-choke collar or harness, but don't hold it. While out and about, call Imp just for the heck of it with your foot on the rope and, if he doesn't Come after three tries, reel Imp in. Whether he Comes on his own or when being reeled, reinforce wholeheartedly. After a week or so, most Imps can be weaned off the rope by lopping off a foot of twine at a time.

Heads up! In dense woods or a crowded dog park Imp's dragging a rope is too cumbersome and potentially dangerous so rehearse elsewhere.

Once Imp is Coming consistently for a week or so, continue to praise his arrivals but now ask him to Sit before offering the treat. Sit defines Come's end and preempts The Drive-by where Imp snags the treats and keeps on traveling.

Reverse Psychology

A wicked little whitewashing-the-fence type trick if wayward Imp refuses to Come When Called is to have him Stay away from you interminably so he begs for the privilege to finally Come.

Let Me Tell You About Kiana, my fifteen-year-old Kuvasz, who was two when I adopted her from her third home. If you don't know Kuvasok, they're a stubborn and independent breed. It was apparent from her utter terror when I first called her that she'd been abused after Coming in one of her prior homes.

Walking my dogs off leash in the woods has always been my greatest joy but, after Kiana ran off one too many times despite my best efforts to train her not to, I resigned myself to keeping her leashed while the others ran free. This broke my heart. Meanwhile, Kiana blossomed with her newfound special status as the only dog lucky enough to be leashed.

Chasing Imp...

... is never a good idea. Not only does it convey that he's the top dog, it teaches him to run away from you. I've known three dogs who were "playfully" chased into oncoming cars. And if Imp has contraband, Chasing teaches him to steal in the future to elicit a Chase, which is at least as good as the gamy old sock he stole. In an emergency, use Imp's Chasefulness to your advantage by running away. Even money he'll run after you.

Go

Though it seems odd to teach Go under Come, passively teaching Imp to Go where he would rather not but must will help to keep Come fresh. Instead of calling Imp to Come into his crate prior to your leaving, say, "Go to your crate" while pointing to it with an underhand gesture. When nearing your house at the end of a walk or if it's time to go inside after playing in the yard say, "Go home." Your Go voice should be upbeat and friendly.

Two Important Reminders

1. The Flight Phase. Around five months puppies spread their wings and, like all teenagers, push boundaries. Imp's independence now does not mean he'll always be unreliable when free, but this is not an age to take chances.
2. Stay and Come are opposite behaviors of equal life-saving importance. Where you stood tall and sounded staccato with Stay; be small and animated with Come. With both Stay and Come, reach under not over Imp's head when contact is made to end the sequence.

Finally, I'd love to promise that these measures guarantee Imp will always Come no matter what, but there are just too many temptations in the real world for that. Like Kiana, some dogs, due to nature and/ or nurture, are simply unreliable off-leash. I do promise, though, that understanding and implementing the above will make your pup as good as he can be. Yours might only be an 85% Coming Imp.

Lie Down

Lie Down can be a pain to teach. If Imp has issues—and who doesn't?—this is where they'll rear their furry heads. For the bossy dog, Down means submit. For the hyper dog, Down means be still. For timid Imp, Down means be vulnerable. That just about covers all dogs.

As you know, there is an active and a passive way to teach everything. Nowhere is the passive approach handier than with

Down. All you need to do is observe Imp in the act of lying Down and say, "Down" while he's in motion. You're labeling the action not the position. To say, "Down" after Imp's been prone for a spell is to label his snoring, scratching, or whatever else he's doing in that moment. If you're able to catch and label Imp lying Down often enough, this may be all that's needed, otherwise...

How To Teach Lie Down

With Imp sitting, hold a bitty treat or choice toy and say, "Down" while lowering your hand from Imp's nose to the floor directly below—underscore, <u>directly</u>. As Imp bends to sniff the treat, slowly inch it away from him and release it once he's fully prone. If Imp paws, mouths or sniffs your treat-holding hand, just keep it in place on the floor until he figures it out. This shouldn't take too long. The time to say, "Down" is when Imp moves himself into position. Remember, we want Imp to own it. In time, the word Down, alone, will motivate the behavior. Pointing to or patting the ground will become the Down hand signal. If bending is difficult, tapping your foot will do.

As with Sit Stay, Down Stay is a two-part exercise. And, as with Sit Stay, some dogs are better at part A and others at B.

Once Imp lies Down without a lot of rigmarole say, "Good Boy, Stay," like it's one word while signaling Stay. Incrementally build up Down Stay with the goal of it being a single, integrated exercise. Practice on Imp's bed in the winter, a cool tile floor when it's hot or anyplace he's comfortable.

Think of Down Stay as an invisible crate. Instead of locking Imp up while you eat or when needing a break from his Impishness, have him Lie Down nearby. Down is your way around begging. Imp may still crave your Mac and Cheese but, as long as he's not in your face, who cares? Rather than leave Imp home alone, a solid Down will enable him to join you at a sidewalk café or when shoe shopping. Much like you'd role-play your acceptance speech in the shower; rehearse each of these scenarios in advance of opening night.

Behaviorally, a strong Down Stay counters dominance challenges and may eliminate mild aggression altogether. However, with the seriously aggressive dog, resistance to the Down is often proportionate to the severity of Imp's aggression. Here, play up the passive approach and seek professional help.

The Send Away (Go Lie Down)

Once Imp has selected his favorite resting spot(s), say, "Go lie down," while signaling the underhanded pointing gesture as he ambles that way. My ReRun summered in the bathtub. When told to Go lie down that's where ReRun planted his 105-pound self.

The Down-And-Dirty of Down

1. After saying and signaled Down, give Imp time to figure it out by holding the treat in your hand on the floor and keeping quiet. Too much talk makes Imp focus on your mouth not your hand. Should Imp paw or mouth your treat-holding hand painfully, wearing work gloves will enable you to stay the course until you are ultimately able to phase-out this step altogether.
2. Rather than hover over Imp, stand or kneel next to him.
3. Try swooping the treat from Imp's nose Down to the floor with finesse. Some Imps enjoy the drama and can be overheard giggling on their way Down.

Controlled Walking

Heel is the proper word for Walking and means, "Walk at my heel." Yeah, sure. I'll explain the more reasonable Controlled Walking here.

For many of us who live in the suburbs with a fenced yard, Walking on leash is a lost art. And I'm thrilled that I don't have to Walk my four dogs every time we step outdoors, but I want to make certain that I can. Like long division, leash Walking is one of those life skills that every well-rounded Imp needs to know.

Dogs naturally Sit, Stay, Lie Down and Come to one another when beckoned, but stifling the urge to dash after a jogger whilst tethered to a string? Not so much. Being completely artificial, Controlled Walking is the one exercise where special training harnesses and collars are often needed. This is not cheating.

The Pros and Cons of *Accoutrement* Choices

All small dogs, and many medium and large ones, should be walked on a harness to protect their delicate tracheas. There are everyday harnesses that are safe but, as with sled dogs, they actually encourage pulling in opposition to the restraint. Then there are training harnesses that prevent pulling but can be a pain to put on and take off a squirming pup. Head harnesses work wonders with many Imps but drive others to distraction and there's a lengthy acclimation period. For sight hounds and other dogs with narrow necks, try a Martingale Collar to prevent Imp's backing out of buckle collars without the danger of a choke collar, something I neither recommend or ever use. While Martingales are perfectly safe, like conventional harnesses, they do little to curb pulling.

I routinely meet people who refuse or delay using a training harness or collar because they view it as a sign of weakness. I explain that even a rhinestoned pink cotton collar, when yanked, could permanently collapse a small dog's trachea.

As for leashes, I appreciate that the retractable kind has advantages in certain situations, but for training, they're too bulky and difficult to control. I recommend a four or six foot cotton, nylon or leather leash.

How To Teach Controlled Walking

Think of Controlled Walking as an efficient way for Imp and you to synchronously—and safely—get from here to there. The perils of walking an unruly ninety-pound Malamute are obvious, but most people don't realize how discombobulating an underfoot Maltipoo can be. I wouldn't be surprised if more injuries result from stumbling over a little dog or getting tangled in his leash than by a big dog's pulling. Imp doesn't know that his actions endanger you—he just wants to chase the squirrel or investigate a scent. Controlled Walking is about teaching him that you're at the other end of the leash and that you'd prefer not to be yanked or tripped.

Traditionally, dogs are taught to walk on the person's left side because—forgive me—the hunter held his rifle on the right. I tend to stick with the left side as there are no sidewalks around here and I like to walk against traffic. This way Imp's on the inside—better I should be run over. Whether you prefer the left or right, select one side and stick with it to avoid getting wrapped-up. Assuming you're a righty and you're walking Imp on your left, hold the leash securely in your right hand and allow it to drape in front of you. Now step away leading with your left leg, pat it and say, "Heel, Let's go, *Andiamo*, Walkies," or whatever. After a few steps, stop and ask him to, "Sit. Atta Imp!" Treat time. With Controlled Walking being a continuous process, there's no defined time to offer a treat. I therefore do so for Sit, a discrete action. Simply knowing that a treat is imminent will keep Imp focused on you. Also, with Sit meaning "I'm in control" you're getting double duty out of the biscuit.

Sally forth again and in a few steps change directions after giving Imp a leg smacking heads-up. If Imp reverses with you, strike up the band. His continuing to walk north despite your having turned south will be met with a self-inflicted Oops! I typically act all surprised here as if to say, "Sorry, buddy, I tried to warn you." The trick to the turnaround is to keep

traveling. Stopping before changing directions blunts the drama. There's nothing like an abrupt direction change to reinforce the benefits of Imp's staying focused on you. And if you'd prefer to simply walk backwards instead of changing direction, be my guest. One more thing, kissing/clicking sounds are universally engaging, so cluck away.

Controlled Walking is only one part of the picture, though. We're not saying Imp can't stop to sniff *anything*—he needs a life, after all— we're simply saying he can't sniff *everything*. Rather than Imp's stopping all willy-nilly, release him by saying, "Okay Imp, be a dog." When it's time to walk, kiss/click/pat/spit and *Andiamo* on your way.

Depending upon how effectively your training collar/harness works, this should be Good Enough for Imp to realize it's worth his while to follow your lead. And, in time, you'll probably be able to phase out the apparatus while still sustaining a Controlled Walk.

Sidebar: For safety's sake, always ask Imp to Sit at the end of your driveway and before crossing all streets. I can think of eight dogs, so trained, whose lives were saved when their leash broke or was dropped. Also, if you walk in a neighborhood without sidewalks as I do, when a car passes urgently whisk Imp over to the side while saying something like, "Out of the road."

Basic Training Troubleshooting

1. If you're certain Imp knows what you're asking but he chooses not to obey, rather than repeat Sit or Stay or Drop It like a fool, after the first failed attempt Correct and Redirect by sharply saying, "No!" then step in close and nicely ask Imp to Sit or Stay or Drop It again. This communicates that not listening is not an option and usually does the trick. The back and forth switching of your voice tone is vital.

2. Don't overdo No! A Correction is meant to end an unwanted behavior not to simply stop it for a moment. If you catch yourself shrieking, No! No! No! check your timing, then nicely redirect Imp and enthusiastically reinforce compliance.

3. A wonderful way to learn how effectively you're communicating with Imp is to test his responsiveness by first issuing verbal cues only and then exclusively through hand signals. Once you determine which he's more responsive to, you'll know which to bank on in an emergency and what needs shoring-up.

4. The Hostess Twinkie Diet. Some people are deeply invested in a particular strategy and so try it over and over again without success. Imp is then deemed "untrainable." I explain that this is like complaining that you didn't lose an ounce after eating Hostess Twinkies for breakfast, Hostess Twinkies for lunch and again for dinner. Mayhaps it's time to try a different diet.

5. Three Strikes You're Out. If you Correct and Redirect Imp three times without success where you had succeeded before, it's time to take a break. Chances are one of you is off. It happens.

6. Direct and Reward or Correct and Redirect. From housebreaking through advanced training, this is the training mantra. Always end on a high and never go to bed angry.

A Word on Practicing

Don't.

Practice evokes piano scales and multiplication tables. Practice is something you get in trouble for not doing. Practice makes perfect. Rather than set fifteen-minutes aside to drill Imp in the den after dinner with a candlestick, weave Basic Training exercises into Imp's day at different times and locations so he effortlessly learns the house rules.

Finally, these No Frills Basic Training exercises are designed for their real-world sustainability and are What Every Imp Needs To Know. Don't do too much too fast and only introduce one new behavior at a time. Once each is understood, go ahead and layer multiple exercises together in a behavior chain. And should you choose to advance Imp's tutelage, No

Frills is also the foundation for agility, search and rescue, therapy work and more.

CHAPTER 12

How To Stop (Really) Annoying Behaviors

I never met a puppy who didn't Jump, Chew or Mouth. If allowed, many dogs will also Bark too much, too. Though these behaviors aren't inherently bad, in excess, they'll drive you mad. Mouthing means on us and Chewing refers to stuff. Here's how to curb these (Really) Annoying Behaviors.

Mouthing

You may have been told that Imp's Mouthing your hand is a precursor to biting and must never be tolerated. I disagree. Puppies Mouth to garner information, much like an infant uses her hands, so the best way to ensure neither turns into Mike Tyson is to teach bite inhibition early on. This can only be accomplished in the context of Mouthing.

Chances are that within moments of meeting infant Imp he'll Mouth your hand. If it's mild, say, "Gentle," to label what's acceptable while keeping your hand still—limp, even. When you've had enough, redirect Mouthing to a toy by presenting it engagingly. If the toy squeaks, squeak it, if it rolls, roll it, etc. Puppies are especially attracted to things that smell (taste?) like us, so season what's legal by first rubbing it to absorb your flavor. And put words to it like, "This is what a good Imp chews." Or you could redirect him to lick instead of Mouth by rubbing a drop of olive oil on your hand and say "Kisses" as Imp licks it off.

If the Mouthing gets too intense, try squealing a high-pitched yip like a wounded littermate might. Your yip should be monosyllabic not sermonic. Done right, Imp will stop Mouthing and possibly cock his head as if to ask, "What the...?" Now remind Imp you're still the boss by asking him to Sit before nicely redirecting him to chew what's acceptable.

Rough play on your part begets rough play on Imp's with Tug of War (TOW) pushing many pups over the edge. I'd therefore avoid TOW in a house with young kids as Imp could go global and tug backpacks off backs or diapers off bottoms. Even in an adult household, TOW with a pushy pup may be too empowering, so play another game.

Dogs are attracted to fast moving objects and go after what's closest. Rather than seductively waving a naked hand in front of Imp's face, hold a toy and he'll aim for it. And limit the amount of sitting-on-the-floor time. This can be especially frustrating for kids so explain that we're doglike on the floor, and there's nothing dogs like more than to Mouth. Standing might be all that's needed to restore decorum.

How much floor time is too much varies from dog to dog. When mild-mannered DJ was a pup, I sat on the floor with him unlimitedly with no ill effect. Cozy is pacified by cuddling at first, but becomes overstimulated quickly, so I gauge our floor time accordingly.

I cannot tell you how often I pay a house call in response to complaints about painful Mouthing and then observe that the complainer's hands never leave the pup. My stock response is to flap my elbow like a funky chicken wing and say, "You know the old joke it only hurts when I do like this? Then don't do like this."

P.S. A client just mentioned that dabbing Vick's VapoRub on her bare feet stopped Bella's toe nibbling altogether. Who knew?

Chewing

There is the career Chewer and your weekend racquetball Chewer; the industrial-strength single object Chewer and one who's equal opportunity. Some breeds are Chewier than others, with retrievers topping the list. (No offense intended, Border Collies herd and Jack Russells bark—no one's Perfect.) Puppies teethe, nonstop, for the first six-months, but the joy of Chewing often exceeds the need to teethe, just like that third Reese's exceeded my hunger.

Regularly Chewed objects include (but are not limited to): Socks, Kleenex, notebooks, Ball point pens, pencils, Magic Markers, crayons, paper towels, paper napkins, cloth napkins, brassieres, pantyhose, clean diapers, dirty diapers, feminine hygiene products, Depends, baseball caps, baseball gloves, baseballs, jock straps, bra straps, Beanie Babies, seat belts, stick shifts, steering wheels, remote controls, disposable razors, nose rings, wedding rings, earrings, toe rings, house plants, bushes, branches, mud, bite plates, patio furniture, kitchen furniture, flip flops, mouse pads, mice, curtains, shower curtains, bath mats, toilet paper, toilet seats, drywall, gloves, mittens, wicker baskets, wicker furniture, eye glasses, sun glasses, fire wood, kindling, matches, cookbooks, coloring books, notebooks, Band-Aids, ace bandages, crutches, cardboard boxes, wood boxes, suitcases, trunks, extension cords, key chains, keys, storm doors...

With all the readily available dog toys, there's no excuse not to indulge infant Imp. A trunk load of playthings is cheaper than replacing one sofa cushion. But don't coat the floors with wall-to-wall toys, as it will make it difficult for Imp to differentiate what's legal from what is not. Six toys at a time, that can be rotated, are plenty.

Sidebar: If you'd like to make your own low-cost, renewable chew toys, rather than stuff a Kong (or the like) with peanut butter as you may have been advised, I'd recommend filling it with Imp's regular rations that are made malleable by soaking in low-sodium broth. This way, there are no empty calories as Imp satisfies his primal urge to get meat off the bone.

Better still, popping it in the freezer will make it last longer while having the added benefit of numbing Imp's sore gums. You can then deduct that much food from the proximate meal. Depending upon how ambitious you are, most or all Imp's calories can be consumed this way.

Let's say you observe Imp gnawing the corner of your kitchen island, snap, "No!" and then immediately redirect him to his best squeaking hedgehog. You may get lucky and this will be the end of it. For the rest of us, if after three failed stabs at Correcting and Redirecting, rather than teach Imp to tune you out, let's change tactics and use that item of attraction to your advantage. Here's what I mean:

Spray that island corner (Nike, mitten, chair leg...) with a Chewing Aversive while strategically placing Imp's hedgehog (Frisbee, Bully stick, stuffed Kong...) nearby so he says, *"Feh!"* upon getting a mouthful of what's *verboten* making what's legit obvious and extra appealing. The beauty part is that, by taking yourself out of the mix, the lesson will endure even in your absence while you retain your innocence. Keep this up for at least five consecutive days until Gestalt is clear: Chewing my stuff is bad; your stuff is good.

And don't be shy about spritzing the Chewing Aversive on your son's shoelaces your daughter's frilly nighty while arming Junior with Imp's best toy to offer as an acceptable alternative.

Chewing isn't just annoying and expensive; it is often deadly. The most serious causes for concern include: The artificial sweetener Xylitol used in many sugarless gums and other products, including some peanut butter brands, grapes and raisins, antifreeze, dark chocolate, medicines, cleaning products, lawn treatments, insecticides and rodenticides. Then of course there's choking and electrocution from chewed wires.

A life-saving number to have handy is the **ASPCA Animal Poison Control Center, 888-426-4435.** This is a 24/7 Service for which your credit card will be charged a fee. Their website is chockfull of useful information, too.

A Word On Aversives

An Aversive is, "An unpleasant stimulus intended to induce a change in unwanted behavior." This could be a sensation, sound, taste or smell. As I trust you've gleaned by now, I am adverse to harsh Aversives and recommend that even a mild one to be used briefly lest Imp becomes desensitized to it. Extreme Chewing and Jumping are potentially life-threatening and are the only two behaviors for which I recommend material Aversives.

Halfway Housing Imp

An easy(ish) way to transition Imp into living with those cherished possessions now off limits is to stage the room with temporary body doubles. Let's say you removed a valuable rug. Rather than simply leave the floor bare, lay down a super cheap rug to be replaced by the real deal once Imp learns not to chew or pee on the surrogate.

I collect tribal baskets. Though they have no great monetary value, they mean a lot to me. With baby Cozy, I replaced the good baskets with some from the Dollar Store and still drenched the cheap ones with the Chewing Aversive while leaving something legal nearby. After a week, I simply left a toy next to the cheap basket without spraying it and after that went well, I replaced the stand-in baskets with the real deal.

A terrific trick to phase out the No Chew spray is to spritz a cologne or other fragrant scent nearby. After a few days, discontinue the stinky stuff while still using the good one in hopes that Imp will now avoid chewing your aromatic hands or fragrant flip flop.

Here's an even more terrific trick I just made up with a test market of one pup, so please don't yell if it doesn't work. I eliminated the No Chew Spray middleman altogether and sprayed cologne on one sock but not its mate. Guess which sock Cozy tiptoed out the door with. The main flaw I foresee with this setup is that your Channel No. 5 probably costs more than the knee-high it's spray on. Back to the drawing board...

Jumping

Jumping's a bitch to fix. I've never met a healthy puppy who didn't Jump. In fact, Jumping is the #1 complaint for which I am called. So let's first look at the anatomy of a Jumper.

As you know, dogs are domesticated wolves. Once weaned, wild wolf pups mull around the rendezvous site with their paws in their pockets poised to Jump and lick their homecoming parents' mouths. In response, the adults upchuck brunch and feed the hungry pups. This food-begging behavior is hardwired for survival.

Fast forward… We spring into action the instant infant Imp Jumps on us, God forbid the little darling's hungry or lonely or in need of a tinkle. By four months, Imp's sprouted wings and we've created a Jumping monster. This is when "we" call me.

The formula to stop Jumping is the same as with all behaviors. First, direct Imp to behave appropriately. Next, reward his compliance or correct the opposite and then immediately re-direct him to what's acceptable. If after three strikes this recipe isn't working, as with chewing, change strategies by using the object of attraction to your advantage. I'll address Jumping on family, guests, neighbors and the kitchen counter separately.

Imp's Jumping on Family

Like his wolf kin, Imp is most apt to Jump during greetings. You needn't return from Iraq for this to be epic, he's just thrilled you're out of the shower. With an up-and-coming Jumper, simply kneel while saying hello so Imp can keep Four-on-the-floor while sniffing your breath for caribou.

If kneeling isn't appealing, or if Imp Jumps at times other than greetings, turn your back to deny the Jump oxygen. Remember, behaviors endure with reinforcement and extinguish without it. Like gravity, this law is non-negotiable. And if you're worried Imp will pee on the floor while your back's turned, weigh the relative merits of missing a possible puddle versus the probability of creating a dangerous Jumper. The window for the back turn to work is brief.

The absence of Jumping is certainly praiseworthy but, lacking form, rewarding the presence of an alternative, incompatible behavior is even better. Pop quiz: Can you guess the best alternative behavior? You got it, good old reliable Sit.

When turning your back isn't enough, in anticipation of Imp's Jumping, step-in smartly to take away the Jump's space. I realize that backing away feels more natural, but retreating invites advances whereas stepping-in often compels a Sit without Imp even knowing what hit him. And if airborne Imp "accidentally" crashes into stepping-in you, at the moment of impact snap, "No Jump!" Now lighten up and ask Imp to Sit, reminding him what he ought to have done. The difference between stepping-in and the old knee-him-in-the-chest camp is that Imp, not you, is the aggressor. If you can't resist the urge to back up, try leaning up against a wall or tree while saying hello. This helps children and genteel grown-ups stand their ground.

Sidebar: If you were told to ignore Imp upon coming home, don't listen. After pining all afternoon for fabulous you, doesn't Imp deserve a calm "Howdy do"? Besides, ignoring him fuels the frenzy with frustration either amplifying his desire to Jump or inviting submissive urination.

For a career Jumper, the kneeling, back turn, step-in ship has sailed. It's time for the (not so) heavy artillery. After 35-years, it embarrasses me that I've yet to find anything more effective than the old can of coins trick. Then again, I still read books on paper, so consider the source. The following should only be used with confident dogs if the preceding measures failed.

No Can Do: Your Problem Solving Kit in a Can

With Imp out of sight, place twenty pennies in a heavy all-metal Can, secure the lid, and leave it by the door. Tea and ornamental Cans work well. Later, enter the room or house as you normally would and shake No Can Do just once mid-jump while saying, "No Jump!" "Off!" or "Are you kidding me?" Put the Can down, step-in close to Imp and nicely ask Imp to Sit. Now offer a treat with your, "Good boy!" Next, change the subject by taking Imp out for a walk or feeding him or tossing a toy. Most dogs dislike the clatter enough that shaking No Can Do two or three times is all it ever takes for them to decide to avoid it. You can now take the pennies out and hold the empty Can the next time you return home. If simply seeing empty No Can Do stops Imp's Jumping, it can be transferred to company and even the kitchen counter. I'll explain how in a minute.

Sidebar: Use a Can that has no other purpose as your No Can Do. We don't want Imp to wince every time you swig a Schlitz.

Imp's Jumping on Company

I've found that people with overly friendly dogs and those whose dogs are unfriendly make the same two mistakes when welcoming guests. First, they take too long to open the front door. Second, after admitting the outsider, they linger by the door too long before moving into the room where they'd normally settle.

The door is Imp's "it" spot. Pizza comes in through the door. Imp goes out the door to play ball. The family returns home through the door and it's the portal of Imp's loneliness and despair. Most Jumps happen near the door. And, because bossy dogs think they own the door, that's where most bites and fights in multiple dog households happen.

More often than not, I ring a new client's doorbell and eavesdrop as Ma (or Pa) feverishly commands Imp to Sit or Stay or Lie Down. By the time the door is finally opened, Imp's all hopped-up, Ma's a mess, I'm covered in snow and our time's almost up. Mortified, Ma now redoubles her efforts to get Imp to Sit or Stay or Lie Down, redoubling Imp's commitment to Jump on me.

Here's how to re-do the how do you do:

1. Don't waste time getting Imp to Sit or Stay or Lie Down before opening the door. His simply keeping all Four-on-the-floor is Good Enough. However, once the outsider is in, a treat is only offered following Sit. If friendly Imp still Jumps after you've taught Imp what No Can Do can do, leave the empty Can outside the door with a little sticky note asking the guest to carry it inside. Because it's empty, no need to worry that the holder will overdo its usage thereby either terrorizing or desensitizing Imp to it. Eyeballing the Can is usually enough to avert a Jump. And remember, Uncle Rudy must put the Can down once its point is made.

2. If you're like me, you hardly ever use the front door. This creates an Oz-like mystique for that rare bird beyond the door either whetting Imp's curiosity or heightening territorial Imp's suspicion. Here, simply de-mystify the front door by having the family occasionally come and go through it, too. If the doorbell's ringing alone gets Imp all crazed, Desensitize while Counterconditioning him to it independent of someone actually being on the other side of the door.

3. Once Rudy is inside, ask him to calmly acknowledge Imp and then lead him into the den where you both sit (and stay). If Imp insists upon nudging or otherwise bugging Rudy, have him rest the (empty) No Can Do on his lap while offering Imp his best toy.

Imp's Jumping on Neighbors When Out and About

If baby Imp Jumps on a passersby, with the 6-foot leash's handle in your right hand, step on the lead so that your foot will keep Imp in place should he try to Jump. This technique works well inside too. It's best to have the leash already on Imp before company arrives. This isn't especially graceful, but with a happy-go-lucky puppy, it'll do for now.

> *Sidebar: Beware of the saboteur. This is the person who, while wearing sweats, says, "I don't mind if Imp Jumps." Trust me, she'll care when in silk.*

Counter-Surfing Imp

This always is serious. Way worse than Imp's pinching your PB&J, the Counter Surfer could steal a steak-encrusted knife, a bunch of (lethal) grapes or sear his feet on the stovetop.

Within a few hours of adopting five-month-old Hodge Podge, I caught him standing on my kitchen counter with his head in a cabinet, chomping on dried pasta in pursuit of the marinara. Not yet knowing the depth of Hodge's commitment, but recognizing that he was remarkably self-assured, I intervened in the following progression over a five-day period.

1. Taught Hodge Podge to Sit and Stay on the floor in hopes of demonstrating appropriate kitchen etiquette. Hodge chuckled at me.

2. Shook No Can Do and left it on the counter. Hodge skirted the Can and camped to its east.

3. Placed a lightweight metal cookie sheet that protruded a few inches beyond the counter's edge with bait just behind it so Hodge would be too spooked to Counter-surf again after the tray he dislodged crashed on the floor. Apparently, I am as dumb as I look.

4. Set up the Bagel Bopper, an entrapment measure that won't hold up in court but works wonders with many clever Imps who wait until you to run to the John to Counter Surf. Here's what to do: tie a string to a bagel (lightly toasted with a smear wouldn't hurt) and tuck the string's other end under No Can Do's lid. Next, place the bagel at the counter's edge with the attached Can pushed back, out of sight. Then casually leave the room and wait for surreptitious Imp to tiptoe over, snag the bagel and run. No Can Do's hitting on the floor, plus Imp's protruding middle finger, will tell you that the Bagel Bopper sting worked.

Sidebar: Beware the brazen Imp who devours the bagel (with a smear) while it's on the counter, thereby reinforcing, not deterring, Counter Surfing. This was the case with Hodge Podge.

5. The Counter Surfer's *coup de grace*: the Scat Mat. These are plastic mats with a battery pack that, when placed on the offended counter top shocks Imp's offending foot. I'm not big on shocking dogs for superficial reasons but, like Invisible-type fences, I believe that a mild, self-initiated zats for over-stepping life-threatening boundaries is a punishment befitting the crime. The Scat Mat was Hodge Podge's undoing.

6. Oh, here's one more set-up that I never actually tried but I've heard works well with select wimpy Imps. Stick two-sided tape along the counter's lip and watch for a peanut-butter-stuck-on-the roof-of-one's-mouth-like response. Not too worry; the tape isn't sticky enough to harm Imp's foot or your counter.

How fast No Can Do, the cookie sheet, Scat Mat or tape can be weaned is the wild card, with two-weeks being a ballpark goal.

Finally, if your pup is just born to Jump, teach him agility Jumps or to leap for a Frisbee or over a high Jump. Like buying the graffiti artist an easel and Acrylics, why not repackage Imp's hobby for good not evil? And if your life just isn't worth living unless Imp Jumps on you, put Jumping on cue by patting your brawny chest while inviting him to Jump. Now that he knows what Jump means, "No Jump" is easier to enforce.

Nuisance Barking

Barking is how Imp expresses himself and his doing so could save your life. Only persistent Barking is considered a problem. Our goal, therefore, is to limit, not eliminate, Barking. With all Imp has to say, let's first look at different Barks.

The Play Bark exists between dogs with one asking, "So you wanna suck face or what?" Imp may also try to engage the cat, vacuum or basketball in this manner.

The Predatory Bark is high-pitched and squealy, and accompanies a rapidly wagging tail.

The Bored Bark drones on and on and on and on...

The Territorial Bark says, "I'm watching you!" Imp's ears are erect, hackles raised and tail held high, making an overall large and in-your-face impression.

The Fear Bark accompanies a retreating or tail-tucked Imp whose ears are usually slicked back.

The Bossy Bark is when Imp looks you squarely in the eyes to demand that you feed or walk or cuddle or lift or toss a ball NOW!

And some dogs are multilingual.

Here's what to do:

Play, Predatory and Bored Barking needs to be managed or tolerated. Play Barking is a byproduct of having multiple critters. With Predation running deep, other than preventing access to prey, I have nothing to suggest. It's time to enrich the Bored Barker's lot.

Territoriality is Barking's double-edged sword. Most dogs display some degree of Territoriality with many selectively bred to protect.

Territorial Barking is often a prelude to biting and requires conscientious management and training.

First, tighten up Territorial Imp's Basic Training, emphasizing Come and Stay, to ensure his responsiveness to voice requests. Next, manage the environment, and Imp's access to it, to thwart Territorial Barking excesses. Here, it helps to understand **The Mailman Syndrome.**

The Mailman trespasses on your property six days a week, Imp Barks and the Mailman leaves. Throw in the paperboy, Mr. UPS, joggers, bicyclists, dog walkers... and the repelling potency of Imp's Bark is reinforced and emboldened throughout the day even when you're away. Then, if an audacious interloper advances despite Imp's best Barking, he's got no choice but to bite Aunt Shirley for disobeying the house rules.

I was hired after two Wire-haired Terriers popped out the window screen and killed a neighbor's Chihuahua. For years, both Terriers wiled their days away perched on the back of a couch by the front window Barking passersby past. When the Chihuahua lingered on their lawn too long, the twosome lunged on the screen as before, but that time it gave way.

This brand of Territoriality, with its attendant Barking, can easily be managed by banning visual access to the stimulus. I suggested the terriers' person simply move the sofa—easy peasy.

Bossy Barking is aimed at you and is a symptom of a relationship out of balance. Just as the bully needs someone who is bullyable, Bossy dogs need a patsy.

First, assert yourself by placing your Bossy Barker on a strict No Free Lunch diet so he pays his way throughout the day with Basic Training. Sit reminds Imp you're in control, with Lie Down being even more controlling, so request both often, prolonging each with Stay. Compliance is non-negotiable.

The opposite of positive reinforcement is not negative reinforcement; it's indifference. To jump out of bed or end a phone call to silence the Bossy Barker benefits him because you were what he wanted. While you are overhauling your relationship with Imp, all Bossy Barking must be ignored.

I know, I know your thinking *I can't let Imp Bark through a business call or bother the neighbors or wake the baby...* This is why you need to role-play indifference when the stakes are low. Let Imp Bark himself silly while you make a fake phone call or when the neighbors are at work and the baby's wide-awake. If the Barking is more than you can bear, use earplugs to stay the course. (I do this when my opinionated parrot, Bugsy Seagull, is on a rant.) To cave-in raises the Barking bar by teaching Imp to be utterly obnoxious to get a rise out of you. Bossy Barking is a gateway behavior that, unchecked, can evolve into Bossy Biting.

With all Nuisance Barkers, teach Quiet (enough, shut up, silencio...) by waiting for Imp to stop Barking on his own and say, "Quiet" after the last Bark. Here, we're labeling the absence of a behavior, which will only make sense in the context of Barking. Once Imp connects Quiet with the end of Barking, hearing Quiet will end his Barking. Now ask Imp to Sit, lavish praise and offer a treat or toss a toy to change the subject.

For the veteran Barker, waiting him out might be too unbearable. Here, an aversive is needed. With all interventions, interrupt the Barking in the gentlest means possible, then immediately re-direct Imp to be Quiet.

Ethical Aversive Options

1. Fill a Plant Mister with cold water and after Imp's informed you that yet another leaf fell in the forest say, "Good boy, quiet." Imp's cocking his head as if to ask, "You talkin' to me?" means he's trying to figure it out. This is a good sign. Hopefully, he'll stop Barking on his own. Otherwise, spritz Imp in the face and, after his last Bark say, "Good boy, quiet." And in case you're wondering about the "Good boy," it's to keep Imp's Barking on retainer if needed to deter wayward solicitors. It helps to know your audience here. A Portuguese Water Dog may respond to the refreshing spray with a, "Thank you very much" and Bark on. But even Hodge Podge, who enjoys swimming and is undeterred by pelting rain, was so startled by the spray that, five-years post-spritz I simply need to show him an empty mister and say, "Quiet" for him to shut up.

Please don't thrust the spray bottle in Imp's face. This may be unduly frightening, creating a new problem.

2. Though **No Can Do** is primarily used to stop Jumping, and it's best to only use it for one problem behavior, but for some Nuisance Barkers a well-timed shake followed by your, "Good boy, quiet" could do the trick. And if Imp's off Barking in the far corner of your yard, fling NCD so the disruptive crash is proximate, as though God dropped it. You're not trying to hit Imp with the Can, just startle him. It's best to tape the lid shut so the pennies don't fly all over giving Imp an opening to mock you.

3. There are a few ethical No Bark Collars worth trying. The first emits an (ostensibly) offensive noise and others spray citronella oil on Imp's chin. While the noisemakers sound great, and they're not terribly expensive, I've never heard of them actually working, though I suppose one might. Citronella Spray Collars are more effective and come in two types. One has a built-in microphone and is activated by Imp's Barking. The other has a remote control so you determine when to spray. The advantage of the Bark-activated collar is that you need not be present for it to work, while the remote-controlled collar enables you to be more selective and can be used to correct behaviors other than excessive Barking.

Finally, all material Aversives have potential side effects and should never be used with timid dogs. Occasionally, seemingly confident Imps react excessively to these setups. If this is the case, discontinue immediately. Even pups who respond respectfully without overreacting may soon become desensitized. The goal, therefore, is to soon replace Aversive usage with a verbal Correct and Redirect.

And to think you were worried about wee-wee.

CHAPTER 13

Deconstructing Common Myths

Dog culture, like all cultures, is steeped in superstition. My mother had told me that feeding bread to my childhood Dachshund, Bell, would give her worms. It never occurred to me to question this until I turned forty. I recently read that no one knows why drinking eight glasses of water is so good for us, or even who made it up, but believing this has been sacrosanct for as long as I can remember.

Many who champion the "unconditional" nature of a dog's love feel betrayed when Imp doesn't measure up. Guilt-ridden clients regularly confess to shameful offenses like feeding Imp "people" food or permitting him on the couch. Feeling more like the wayward priest than Mother Teresa, I offer absolution by admitting similar lapses with my own flock while wondering when puppy rearing became so parochial.

Never Permit Imp on Furniture

Though there are tons of reasons why Imp shouldn't be allowed on the sofa, and I would never actually prescribe it, there's one compelling reason to permit him: it's yummy. Worry not, it is possible to let Imp on the ratty old den couch but not the damask living room one. And if Imp's

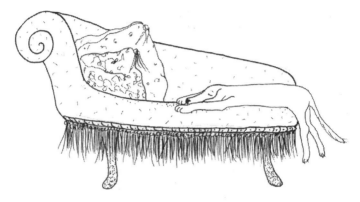

filthy, it's even possible to selectively keep him off the tacky one. Here's how:

Place a sheet, blanket or towel on the floor and pat to invite Imp on it while saying something like, "On your blankey." Sitting on it yourself will make it even more appealing. Now drape the blanket over the couch and invite Imp on it there. Floor/couch. Floor/couch. Floor/couch. Where the blankey is Imp can sleep. Neat, no?

Heads Up! Occasionally, Imp feels too empowered or territorial on the furniture and becomes aggressive. When my late husband returned from a business trip, our dog, Plain Jane, resented being ousted from "her" side of the bed and snarled if Marc got too close. PJ always came around after 24-hours, so Marc and I simply sequestered her during our happy reunions.

Don't Feed Imp "People" Food

This makes me nuts. And what does it even mean? Is corn a people, pig or dog food? Is fresh chicken less healthful than the chicken by-product meal in many commercial diets? Of course, plenty of the foods we eat are dangerous for dogs, but if you are ambitious enough to research canine nutrition and decide to either feed Imp exclusively fresh foods or to supplement his commercial diet with them, as long as you introduce new foods slowly, I'd go for it.

Some worry that feeding Imp our food will encourage begging. True, if you offer Imp *pâté* from your plate he'll hit you up for more. It is also true that slipping him kibble at the dinner table will do the same. Where the food is offered is the problem, not the food itself.

Show Imp Who's Boss by Making Him Eat After You

The rationale here is that alpha wolves get first dibs of the prime ribs with the spoils left for the underlings—a notion that's simply not so. Still, there's nothing wrong with Imp's eating after you. However, given the average family's non-stop noshing, I can't help but wonder whether implementing this is worth the *agita*.

Imp Must Follow You Through Doors

In case you haven't heard, the ultra controlling contend that Imp's preceding you through a door must never be tolerated as it's a prelude to his joining the Crips. I do agree that it's best not to let the super pushy bolt past but, in the hierarchy of things to worry about, enforcing this across-the-board is tantamount to banning all milk products in kindergarten on the off chance little Johnny could possibly be lactose intolerant.

Cheating

I had a lengthy conversation with a soft-spoken southern social worker whose wheelchair-bound partner was just diagnosed with Alzheimer's and whose four-month-old Cockapoo begs during dinner. The caller claimed that her partner "forgets" that she shouldn't feed Roxy from the table, though it sounded to me like she simply enjoyed doing so. After listening to the litany of aggressive ambush strategies employed to quell the begging "once and for all," I asked why, with so much on her plate, she didn't simply crate Roxy during dinner for now. The social worker responded, "But I thought that was cheating."

Unconditional Love

A dog's love is revered to be uniquely Unconditional, superior to Conditional Love with all those strings attached. And people seem deeply invested in this belief, often citing Imp's disinterest in their flabby thighs or questionable breath as proof of his Unconditionality, though it simply proves a lack of superficiality. Unconditional Love loyalists think they're respectful. I don't: I think it's self-serving and sets Imp up to fail.

Conditions imply reciprocity. I do for you on the Condition that you do for me. Conditions are the glue that makes a relationship work. Clients often complain that Imp will only listen if "there's something in it for him." My stock response is, "I'm only here because you're paying me." So it is with Imp.

Dogs' Conditions differ from ours in their nature and timing only. Lacking ambition, Imp doesn't suck up today to reap benefits tomorrow: he just wants to make the most of this moment. But don't devalue the simplicity of these Conditions, they're as potent and as necessary as yours or mine.

The belief in Unconditional Love turns sinister when Imp's acting up is seen as an intentional affront. A client said, "Unconditional Love my ass, Rex knew those were my favorite boots and chewed them to spite me for staying out late." This sentiment, though idiotic, is more common than you may think.

Spite is about getting even with someone in the present for a past offense to prevent its reoccurrence in the future. This transcendence of past/present/future time zones is a complex computation that exceeds Imp's math skills.

I propose that whenever Imp's acting-out seems motivated by spite, substitute "stress" and it will wash. Either way, the boots are toast, but stress evokes sympathy where spite sounds diabolical, often justifying an equivalent response.

Though not technically a myth buster, something just occurred to me. While I staunchly defend my belief in the Conditional nature of a dog's love, perhaps what's confusing is that dogs are nonjudgmental. This, I agree, is laudable.

Possible/Probable: Naked Imp

To keep me from overreacting when young, my father would ask, "Is it Possible or Probable?" Thereafter, "Possible/Probable" was code to keep things in perspective. A common Possible/Probable conundrum is whether or not to leave a collar on Imp. Trivial though this may seem, it's anything but.

I teach group classes at an Animal Hospital on a busy road and I tell everyone upfront that Imp should arrive at class wearing a buckle-type collar or harness and they must be on leash before exiting the car. I also make clear that choke collars are not permitted. Still, every first class a puppy or two flies out of the car, untethered. The most popular explanation is, "What if the leash gets tangled in the car?" to which I answer, "What's worse, the slight Possibility that Imp will be unable to stretch for the short ride to class or his running into the Boston Post Road?"

Some people are afraid that the collar will get caught on the furniture or in the crate, which is Possible, but only dangerous if Imp's wearing a choke collar. Being collarless, Imp has nothing but flesh or fur to grab hold of in an emergency, causing many dogs to bite, and there's nothing to affix an ID to. As any Animal Control Officer will attest, dogs that scoot out doors without identification fill most Pounds. After thirty-five-years, and thousands of dogs, I have never heard of one getting into trouble wearing a non-choke collar but know of many who went missing without.

Anthropomorphization

To Anthropomorphize is to attribute human traits to non-humans (because we're so great). Though this is meant to be flattering, I see it differently.

As I mentioned in my first book, *Rover, Don't Roll Over*, a client once said, "I love my dog, I just hate when she does doggy things." This reminded me of Henry Higgins asking, "Why Can't a Woman Be More Like a Man?" A current client is eager to have her Papillion play with other dogs so long as there's "no chewing, sniffing or chasing." This would be funny but for her kicking any pup who solicits play at the dog park.

Now you'll never catch me using the word "just" when referring to a dog, but to Anthropomorphize implies that Imp isn't Good Enough as is. Like the westerner admiring an Asian's Anglicized features or the African's processed hair, how narcissistic are we?

I just spoke to a man who opened the conversation by saying, "Jessie is not a dog, she's a person." This was repeated four times. My, "sounds like you don't like dogs" dig was wasted on him.

Alpha Schmalpha

Being Alpha, a concept borrowed from wolf culture, crept into dog parlance a few decades back, promising a softer system to replace the totalitarian Germanic paradigm of training. So far: so good. No sooner did Alpha set up shop than many manipulated it to justify a New Age of abuse. With exploitation abounding in Alpha's name, here is what Alpha actually means.

Alpha wolves are the head of a given pack. This is an absolute distinction like being Pope, president or pregnant. Amongst wild wolves, the Alphas are the parents and their pups make up the nuclear pack. In-laws and other extended family members often help out with babysitting and chores. There aren't gradations of Alphaness, you're Alpha or you're not. Alpha wolves are born not manufactured and are neither bullies nor tyrants; they are simply doing their job. Alpha-ers or Alpha-ests need not apply.

CHAPTER 14

Things You Can't Control

No matter how hard we try, there are certain really annoying dog behaviors we humans can't completely control. Here are a few.

Having A Hairy

Ever witness young Imp scoot, as if possessed, while muttering expletives before blacking-out? This is a Hairy (not from the Latin). My take on the Hairy is it's over-tired Imp's releasing residual energy, like a jet dumps fuel before an emergency landing.

As alarming as a Hairy is to watch, it's harmless. When Cozy's fried, she'll whimper or chase her tail or insist upon nibbling my arm despite my asking her not to, like she just can't help herself. Now that I've identified this as an early-onset Hairy, I either preempt the lunacy at its inception by tossing a treat in her crate knowing she'll follow it in and be snoring in moments, or I allow the Hairy to play itself out. Like thumb sucking, the Hairy is primarily a youthful concern.

Rolling in Stinky Stuff

Is there anything more disgusting than Imp's rolling in poop or a dead animal? And why do they always go down neck first? There are a few theories as to why dogs roll, all residual wolf behaviors.

One theory claims the predator rolls to mask his own scent so Bambi doesn't smell him coming. Forgive me, but since when does a doody mound move? The second theory says the wolf is claiming the decomposed elk with scent glands on his neck. It's hard to imagine those secretions overpowering the stench of rotting flesh, but I suppose it's possible. The third suggests he's bringing the scent back to the pack to flaunt his booty. And the final theory is that he just likes to roll.

Other than preventing access to Stinky Stuff, I have no solution. However, if Imp rolls as if to put the stink back following a fragrant bath, he may be trying to mask the girly scent, so use an odorless shampoo.

Digging

Here, I may be able to help you a little but I don't make any promises. There are many reasons dogs dig: the terriers and dachshunds were selectively bred to "Go-to-ground." Hot dogs dig to unearth cooler dirt. The roamer or romantic dog digs to escape. Anxious Imp digs as a  stress reliever, the hoarder to cache a bone, and the bored dog because there's nothing better to do.

1. For the hot dog, provide a hard plastic kiddy pool, a marble slab or another means to cool off.
2. Time to have romantic Imp snipped, and shore-up the fence.
3. For the others, legalize digging by providing a Designated Dig Spot (DDS). Pick a mutually agreeable DDS area where Imp's shown interest and that you can live with aesthetically without twisting an ankle. Take a hunk of meat or a dog-safe bone, march

over to your DDS, trowel in hand, dig a hole and bury the treasure in it, real matter-of-factly. No need to call Imp or actively engage him, he's on to you. The second he begins digging up your haul, rave, "Atta boy, Imp! This is where a good boy digs. Give me an I..." Repeat. Repeat. Repeat, Repeat, Repeat... In time, upon spotting that digging glint in Imp's eye, say, "Yo Imp, where does a good boy dig?" And, God willing, he'll show you. This worked with my Buddha who has been mining her well for fifteen years. I replenish the dirt every spring and by October she could bury an Escalade in it.

Thunder Storm Phobia

This is a toughie. Because phobias are, by definition, irrational, attempts to convince Imp that those flashing lights and resounding booms are harmless fall on deaf ears. Some dogs are freaked from their first storm and others, like my eight-year-old DJ, develop the phobia when a wayward clap rattled the roof. Symptoms are similar to those of Separation Anxiety with some afflicted dogs seeking consolation while others retreat into the closet or bathtub.

With a brand new baby Imp, your acting calm and happy before and during a storm wouldn't hurt. And if you have your own storm issues, please get a grip. I love a good storm but my old girl, Kiana, dissolves into a gelatinous mound of white fur the instant the wind picks up. Storm Phobias are managed not cured. Here are some coping strategies that are also applicable to fear of fireworks:

1. Offer natural remedies like melatonin, Rescue Remedy or Phosphorous PHUS 30c in anticipation of a storm. My friend Hazel swears by melatonin.
2. Turn on the AC and lower the blinds.
3. Play music or break out the sousaphone.
4. Swaddling soothes some Imps. Thunder Shirts and other commercial dog wraps are readily available.

5. The bathtub: Old Mowgli was the first of my dogs to climb into the tub during a storm and I thought it was a cute quirk. Then ReRun did the same. Next, Stinky. And clients report their dogs also do this. (A plumber once explained why this works but I forget.) Encourage large Imp to climb in the dry tub or place little Imp in and see if it calms.

6. In the hardcore cases where Imp literally climbs the walls, consult your vet. A tranquilizer may be necessary.

When a Beloved's Successor Doesn't Measure Up

I'm not sure this belongs here, but I just paid a house call that hammered home its importance, so here goes:

All too often, after a treasured dog dies, his people race to "replace" him with a similar dog. The problem is that Senior was one of a kind and even though Junior is also a Springer Spaniel, he's still his own person. This is especially insidious if the first dog died unexpectedly or when the name is passed down.

Over the phone, Shasta 2's elderly Ma didn't have a kind word to say about the nine-month-old puppy. The woman went so far as to call Shasta a, "lemon" and "evil." So I arrived at their house braced for The Exorcist but was welcomed by Orphan Annie.

After my umpteenth reassurance that Shasta's behavior was "perfectly normal," Ma revealed that Shasta1 had been killed by a coyote when left outside unsupervised. Though I understood the guilt and disloyalty Ma felt, I pointed to the puppy who eyeballed her adoringly and said, "But it's not her fault." This did the trick.

CHAPTER 15

Why Imp Bites

Dogs bite for a bunch of reasons, some health related, others environmental, most, behavioral. On the health/ environmental front, management's the name of the game. Supervise your toddler so she doesn't pounce on the Shepherd's painful hip. Prevent your territorial Giant Schnauzer from greeting Mr. UPS before you do. Flicker the lights or slam the door so the vibration will alert a deaf Dalmatian you're approaching. And never blanket a dense-coated Samoyed in August. If your usually friendly dog shows inexplicable aggression, have your vet check him out. An ear infection or hypothyroidism, amongst other ailments, could be responsible.

Behaviorally, the reasons dogs bite are more complex. Dominant aggression is typically directed at a family member and fear-based aggression is aimed at outsiders, though sensitive Imp will nail his own overbearing people if bullied. The fear-biter needs to be built up, the bossy biter, toned down. This formula is too simplistic to take to the bank, but more often than not it's accurate. People living with dogs at both extremes need guilt-free empowerment.

I have learned to be suspicious of the labels assigned a behavior, especially where safety's concerned. Because Imp's behavior is often misinterpreted, as was the case with Chauncey, or his people lie or are in denial about what happened, I ask that the behavior be described in terms of what is seen, heard or felt. But first, let's look at Hand Shyness.

Hand Shyness

The Hand Shy pup flinches as if about to be hit no matter the hand's intention. Observing this, prior abuse seems certain. But even dogs reared under ideal conditions frequently shrink away when an unfamiliar hand abruptly reaches over his head. This reaction goes deep.

Between dogs, one placing his head or paw over another's head is viewed as a dominance challenge. If the underdog deems the overture innocent, a play session follows; otherwise there may be a fight.

Strays are especially susceptible to Hand Shyness, either because they'd been harshly shooed away—or worse—or if spooked by a well-meaning rescuer's attempt to capture them. When cornered, a fearful dog bites the offending hand. Had the person reached under, not over, Imp's head, chances are the bite would never have happened.

But not all Hand Shy dogs are of uncertain upbringing. I paid a house call after Ma's hand was badly bitten by a 10-month-old Old English Sheepdog, Chauncey, who was relegated to a cold mudroom with a dog door leading to a small pebble yard. This is where Ma and I stood discussing the shaggy show dog's fate. Ma explained that Chauncey had been growling for months when she dried him and that it recently escalated "for no reason whatsoever."

I soon observed that every time Chauncey passed through the dog door or sipped water, Ma scoured his dew-moistened feet or mouth with such rigor the woman even scared me. Chauncey didn't get that Ma was mad at the wet; he thought she was mad at him. I explained Fight, Flight and Freeze and that fear is the main reason dogs bite. The diminutive quarters precluded Flight, so when Freeze's warnings were ignored, Chauncey (believed he) had no choice but to bite her.

To remedy Hand Shy Imp, Desensitize/Counter Condition him with treat-toting/toy-tossing hand gestures that incrementally intensify in grandiosity. Stretch with gusto and sneeze with pizzazz. Swing your arms playfully while ignoring winces and reinforcing self-confidence. After the naked hand is tolerated, gradually integrate a towel, broom or top hat into the process. Chauncey's rehabilitation is more certain than Ma's.

Hand Shyness in previously traumatized dogs rarely goes away completely. Eight-year-old DJ, who purrs through his twice-daily injections, just blanched when I snatched a cereal box off the top shelf.

Denial and Other Lies People Tell
The Lie: Big Tooth

At least once a week a client swears that this is the very first time Imp ever jumped or mouthed or growled or bit or... Now, I recognize a budding behavior from one that's entrenched, making me want to scream, "How dumb do you think I am?" Of course, lying about a Bichon Frise's playful jumping is more forgivable than lying about a St. Bernard's biting. The latter recently happened.

I was suspicious when the mother-in-law called and claimed that 200-pound Big Tooth "nipped." Because "nip" is one of those nebulous words that often refers to a puppy's playful mouthing, I asked her to clarify what "nip" meant. A muffled, "He-nipped-the-housekeeper-in-the-face-and-she-lost-part-of-her-nose" snuck out. Still, I paid a house call hoping to unearth the extenuating circumstance for this isolated incident.

Big Tooth's parents, the mother-in-law, nanny, landscaper, housekeeper and driver were all present, each expressed strong, often opposing, opinions. That's when the nanny admitted that the nose "nip" was actually the last straw in a series of lesser bites. Presumably, the mother-in-law deemed withholding this critical detail a "fib."

I explained that dog culture is not run by committee and there needed to be one chief who the other players supported. Next, we went over No Free Lunch, emphasizing Big Tooth's earning his way through absolute adherence to Basic Training. For the program to work, everybody had to be on board.

Denial: Zanzibar

The line between lying and denial is often blurred, with denial easier to justify than a boldfaced lie. Often, caring adopters deny their newly rescued dog's poor behavior. I understand this and feigned all, "she-never-did-that-before" when Cozy made off with the adorable tree guy's leather glove. Looking the other way with garden-variety naughtiness is no biggy, but where safety's concerned, noses get et.

I had worked with Robert and his first Rhodesian Ridgeback, Razor, who became a model citizen. Then Robert adopted another Ridgeback through rescue. Feeling badly about Zanzibar's checkered past, Robert set no boundaries and was in denial about the dog's escalating aggression until Zanzibar bit his niece. While I don't believe in one size fitting all, I was able to convince Robert that the disparity in his treatment of the two dogs handicapped Zanzibar thereby enabling his aggression.

Little Big Dog

Though it's not fair, Big and Little Dogs are held to different standards. A Big Dog's bite is bigger and his jump, more powerful. Little Dogs bite more often and I find that their bark is way more grating. A Big Dog hogs up more of your bed but a Little Dog can burrow beneath the sheets, owning them. Ever hear that Little Dogs can't be housebroken? I guarantee you that if a Little Dog's puddles and piles were as massive as a Big Dog's, he'd be housebroken lickety-split.

Dog breeds are manmade contrivances designed for our exploitation—I mean, pleasure. Herders were invented to round up rogue sheep, pointers broadcast the pheasant went thataway, guard dogs keep the perimeters secure and terriers ferret out rats. Then there's an enormous group of elite little dogs whose soul *raison d'être* is to sit on one's lap. These surrogate

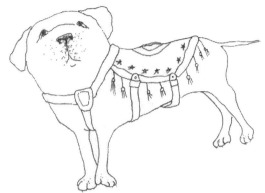

babies frequently have infantilized features and health restrictions that guarantee their perpetual dependency.

I originally identified The Little Dog Syndrome in response to another nose bite. That time, Precious, an eight-pound Maltese, took her Ma's nose all the way off when the elderly woman crawled beneath the bed to retrieve a pilfered hanky. This brand of object guarding harkens back to a wolf caching uneaten reindeer for a rainy day, and it's a uniquely Little Dog event because—duh!—Big Dogs don't fit beneath the bed. Princess, like any self-respecting wolf, believed she had no choice but to fend off Ma's wanton invasion of her den.

Precious began barking the instant I rang the doorbell and continued through the first half-hour of our session as Ma clutched the quivering creature to her bosom. My suggesting she place Precious on the floor clearly baffled Ma, like it had never occurred to her. Once demoted from the "there, there" perch, Precious stopped barking while nervously searching for her land legs.

Precious' portability handicapped her in two important ways. First, because she was carried hither and yon, Precious never learned the rules of the road. Second, the nonstop holding made Precious especially receptive to Ma's insecurities and neediness. With the nose bite symptomatic of a relationship out of balance, our priority was to establish a serviceable equilibrium between the coddling that Little Dog parents crave and the respect No Free Lunch engenders.

I suggested that Ma pretend Precious weighed 80-pounds and we taught her Basic Training exercises with four paws on the floor, emphasizing Sit as a reminder that Ma's in charge. Next, I put Ma on a "cuddle diet" and instructed her to offer hugs sparingly and only for a job well done. Finally, I explained that Ma's hands and mouth had to be on the same page. To fondle Precious while saying, "Stop that, Sweetie," taught her to ignore Ma's mouth and listen to her hands. Precious was still permitted, by invitation, to watch TV on Ma's lap and she could hold Precious for up to two-hours a day.

I believe we have the relationships we want. Ma wants to pamper Precious; she just doesn't want to get bit. By establishing Little Big Dog ground rules, we created a Good Enough compromise that's safe.

A Tale of Two Sidneys

I probably shouldn't tell you this, but an awful lot of my clients are stricter than I am. It seems that those most out of control of their own behavior overcompensate by micromanaging Imp's. Let me tell you about Sidney, the 140-pound Great Dane-mix.

I arrived at Sidney's home knowing that he had recently bitten a female guest and he'd begun snarling at passersby on walks. Sidney waited inside the screen door watching me fiddle with the jerry-rigged front gate while Ma barked, "Sit, Sidney! Damn it, Sit!" and, "I'm coming, Jody! I'm coming!" This created a ton of tension, delaying *détente* for a good five minutes. By the time Sidney and I finally met, he was in a lather—literally—and so agitated I suspect anybody else would have been bitten. Meanwhile, once I stepped into the kitchen and sat, Sidney draped his slobbery snout over my shoulder. He had simply been reacting to Ma's anxiety that communicated my protracted entrance was a worrisome thing. At both ends of the greeting spectrum—too friendly or not so much—stepping away from the entranceway diffuses the intensity. Also essential with Sid, Ma needed to repair the gate for briefer, less stressful arrivals.

Later, while Ma and I walked Sidney around the neighborhood, a woman asked if she could greet Sidney whose demeanor flipped from approachable to guarded the instant Ma tensed on the leash cautioning the woman to "stay back" before snapping, "Sit, Sidney! Damn it, Sit!" With that greeting already sullied, I took the leash and acted all happy happy when another neighbor neared as Sidney wiggle-waggled in kind. I then asked Sidney to Sit and handed the woman a treat to offer him, explaining that simply dropping the biscuit on the ground would suffice for now as she seemed uneasy. Next, I armed the neighbor with a bunch of biscuits to take home for her husband and each of her three teenagers to individually replicate the greeting. Other than Sidney's sliming everyone, each greeting was 100% appropriate.

When Ma questioned my not insisting Sidney Sit prior to permitting outsiders to approach, I explained my Four-on-the-floor principle that, as long as Sidney's demeanor is relaxed and he doesn't jump, there's no need to delay greetings awaiting Sit. However, Sit is necessary to earn a cookie. Hairsplitting though this sounds, the behavioral shift is seismic.

A Word on Timing and Treats: It is vital that the delivery of treats be well timed. Remember, Reinforcement must be offered immediately following the targeted behavior. To offer a treat mid-menace in hopes of sweetening Imp's sour mood actually rewards the menacing. When uncertain about the timing, it's best to withhold treats altogether lest you make matters worse.

Proactive vs. Reactive

There seems to be two kinds of (dog) people: those who want to preempt a problem from developing and others who prefer to wait until one hits critical mass before addressing it. The Proactive camp leans towards positive reinforcement; the Reactive, negative reinforcement. Being of the Positive Proactive Persuasion, I am endlessly shocked by how long some people delay getting help.

I just hung up with Vivian, whose six-year-old Wheaton Terrier has seriously hurt four dogs, including her other Wheaton. Vivian casually added that Spike also bit three people. She then asked if we could meet at the dog park so I could, "see Spike in action." I explained that I don't need to witness Spike maul another dog or person, nor do I need to be bitten to be effective. Proactively recreating a provocative situation (with safeguards in place) would be the swan song of Spike's rehabilitation for which we must rehearse.

Nature Abhors a Vacuum

As dissimilar as the above examples seem, each illustrates a leadership vacuum that enabled Chauncey, Big Tooth, Zanzibar, Precious, Sidney and Spike to seize control. Establishing a strict No Free Lunch regimen of consistent boundary-setting Basic Training was all it took to create balance. With severe aggression, please seek professional help.

An Aggression-Begetting-Aggression Afterthought

A prospective client with a recently adopted ten-month-old shepherd-mix asked, "Is it ever okay for a dog to bite its master?" I found that an odd question with the, "its master" especially telling. He went on to explain that the bite followed his, "holding the pup down and smacking him for scratching the door." I responded, "If a dog feels legitimately threatened when flight is impossible and freeze has proven ineffectual, then yes, I do believe a dog has a right to bite." That the law might see it differently was not mentioned.

CHAPTER 16

Kids and Imps

D on't get a dog for your ten-year-old. Please, don't. Get a dog because you want one and hope Junior feels the same.

And don't think your ten-year-old is going to take "full responsibility" for Imp. Please, don't. I've seen a prison guard, captains of industry, psychoanalysts, mothers of multiples and others brought to tears by a recalcitrant pup's antics. If puppies weren't so much work I wouldn't be so busy, thank you very much.

Do get a dog because life's essential lessons—compassion, generosity, sharing, tenderness, loyalty, accountability and consequences— can be learned through living with one. Unquestionably, the best things about me came from growing up with animals. But your Kids needn't be as over-the-top as I was for Imp to be a life-defining addition, especially today.

In our overscheduled, high tech world, time with Imp may be Junior's only non-mechanized outlet. Rather than allow the relationship to unfold organically, Type A parents often micromanage the magic right out it. But Kids, like the rest of us, want to fall in love of their own free will. As with love of music or sports or cooking, love of animals should be fostered not force-fed. Nothing kills passion more completely than ramming piano lessons down one's throat.

Before Bringing Imp Home

It is natural to fear what we don't understand and to avoid stuff that makes us feel stupid, so study up in anticipation of Imp's homecoming and if there's somebody like me handy, have her over to personalize expectations and age-appropriate tasks for each Kid. Perhaps your nine-year-old prepares Imp's meals and the six-year old places the bowl on the floor. One twin walks Imp after breakfast and the other after dinner. Your only child could select from a list of tasks.

Puppies have two gears—destructo and comatose. These extremes can easily overwhelm and disappoint Kids. Rather than paint over the rainbow possibilities, I'd lowball expectations while emphasizing that, unlike Junior's baby cousin, Imp's infancy will fly by in a matter of months.

Agree upfront about how much time Junior can sit on the floor with Imp and explain the Let Sleeping Dogs Lie law. What often happens is, because the awake puppy is such a pest, Kids (and lots of adults) are attracted to him while asleep in hopes the calm will endure. It won't.

While negotiating the house rules, keep your Kids engaged by using their strengths to ready the house and yard for Imp's arrival. Budding Picasso could adorn the environs with welcome home banners. The builder might construct a ramp or maze. Your baker could make bone-shaped biscuits.

Explain that baby Imp is a chewing machine. If your Kids are old enough to put their belongings away and don't, as long as Imp doesn't have access to anything sharp or toxic or small enough to choke on, use his destroying their stuff as a teachable moment. Same with cleaning up Imp's mess on the wall-to-wall because Junior dilly-dallied texting.

From Homecoming through No Frills Basic Training, find fun, age-appropriate ways to engage your Kids in all aspects of Imp's upbringing. Though tricks aren't my thing, they're a great way to involve Kids.

Good Enough Tricks

1. Wag your tail if you're a good dog is an excellent entry-level crowd pleaser. All that Junior needs to do is hold a treat and, in her sing-songiest voice, say, "Wag your tail if you're a good dog." Imp will be all too eager to oblige.

2. Slap me five is irresistible to most Kids. Here, Junior holds a treat in her fist and presents it to Imp who will try and try to make that treat materialize by mouthing, whining and, hopefully, pawing Junior's hand. Mid-smack Junior says, "Slap me five" and then releases the prize.

3. Capitalizing on Imp's quirkiness is usually good for a laugh. Cozy always does this little spinning dip when asked to Lie Down, so I signal Down but say, "Curtsey."

4. Jump through a Hula Hoop is easier than you'd think. Wedge a standard-sized Hoop in standard-sized doorway, flush with the floor. Junior now tosses balls or treats through the Hula Hoop and as Imp steps through it, Jr. says, "Hup." And if two kids want to get involved, calling Imp back and forth through the Hoop adds another layer of excitement. With an adult's permission, the Hula Hoop is left jammed in the doorway and, once Imp is comfortable just walking through it, raise it a few inches a day saying, "Hup" as Imp actually jumps. From here, Junior's directing Imp to Hup through a handheld Hula Hoop is a hop, skip and a jump away. Of course, if Imp is frightened of the hula-hoop, try another trick.

5. Roll Over Rover, don't.

Junior's Attention-Seeking Behaviors

When a parent claims that Imp and Junior are always butting heads, as parents often do, I wonder who gains most from the disharmony.

A mother phoned because the puppy and Sam, her six-year-old son, were so adversarial that they were seriously thinking about rehoming Max (the pup). Ma mentioned that she and her husband had recently separated and they adopted Max to "soften the blow." She believed that Sam's acting out was a function of his resenting the pup's "replacing" his dad. I agreed that this was probably part of it, and noted Ma's rapid-fire refereeing of the twosome that punctuated our twenty-minute conversation.

I paid a house call the following week and within minutes observed a mischievous glint transform Sam's face as he needled the puppy, knowing full well that Max would turn around and nail him. As expected, Ma leapt up from the table to intervene and lecture Sam (for what I assume was the umpteenth time) not to bug the pup who was banished to the crate (for what I also assume was the umpteenth time). Sam soon began needling Max inside the crate, causing Ma to race over and say, "See what I mean?" Yep, I saw.

That's when I gave the "behaviors need reinforcement to endure" spiel and suggested that the secondary gains of her snapping-to after each episode actually fueled the conflict. Ma responded by saying, "But all I do is yell at Sam."

Bingo!

The notion that negative reinforcement is still reinforcing is hard for many to digest. Clearly, we'd all prefer to be hugged than hollered at, but if the hollering is the only or primary attention one gets, it's better than nothing. Ma seemed willing to accept this as an explanation for the pup's acting up but was oblivious to it also motivating her son.

I suggested that we repackage Max and Sam's relationship by first selecting bite-sized tasks with the specifics enumerated that were easy enough for both to succeed and challenging enough for each to feel proud.

Ma needed to enthusiastically cheerlead both players successes thereby precluding—or at the very least, minimizing—negative attention-seeking behaviors. We agreed that Sam would feed Max breakfast and he'd toss the ball for Max fifteen times a day during the week and thirty times on weekends. Sam and I then taught Max to Sit and Stay and I asked Sam to select a trick. He picked Slap Me Five. No surprise.

Kids and Imps getting along is a beautiful thing. If Junior chooses to hang back at first, let it be. I frequently see late bloomers come around on their own time. And some don't. With so much at stake, by establishing Good Enough guidelines, Lassie and Timmy just might happen. Good luck!

CHAPTER 17

Introducing Resident Imp To Baby

In anticipation of Baby's birth, acclimate Imp to infant paraphernalia and likely lifestyle changes, one at a time while you still have your sanity. Whether adding a crib or phasing out the midnight romp, give Imp five days to get used to each (major) change before introducing another. It typically takes six weeks for dogs to own a new pattern, so get cracking.

You've probably heard about wrapping a doll in a blankey and playing a recording of a crying Baby and even borrowing a poopy diaper—all good. Because Imp will pick up on your energy, act relaxed and happy while burping your swaddled, diaper-clad Chatty Cathy.

The more Imp is included in Baby-centric activities the better. Build up Imp's Down Stay muscle so he can be close while Baby is fed or changed or napping. Work on the Send Away to demonstrate an acceptable option if Imp needs a break. Practice Imp's Controlled Walking beside a carriage carrying Chatty Cathy so she, not Baby, is ejected while ironing out the kinks.

Assuming Imp is curious but not overly excited by the ersatz infant, if you know someone with a test Baby to invite over, do so. Imp needs to be on a leash for the introduction. Rather than snap the leash on once the doorbell rings (and all hell to breaks loose), take Imp out for a walk ahead of time and then simply let go of the leash where the introduction will happen so it is already in place if needed.

It's best to introduce Baby and Imp in a neutral spot outside the house or apartment. The front yard, garage or lobby will do. Walk Imp over to Baby, whose face is shielded by the holder and, as long as Imp's under control, he's welcome to sniff her. After a relaxed Howdy-do, enter the house, Baby first. As with all greetings, step away from the door. Imp can now smell Baby as before but this time Baby "hands" Imp a special toy or safe chew bone. By getting the sniff-and-greet out of the way fast, you deemphasize the magnitude of this alien being's presence. Hopefully, Imp will find Baby's gift engaging enough to go off with it.

Sidebar: I would assume that only a relaxed parent would volunteer her infant for this experiment. However, as the handler's energy is integral to the success of the Introduction, be selective about who you ask to participate. It's better to skip this step altogether than proceed under duress.

Bringing Baby Home

Whether Baby is adopted by a single parent or born to a same-sex couple, the introduction particulars are the same. Simply shift Ma and Pa and the pronouns around and follow along.

Make sure that Imp is well-exercised on the day of Baby's homecoming. A little Rescue Remedy or a calming supplement wouldn't hurt. Because Ma will look, smell and act differently than when she left, or perhaps she's been a way for a while, she should go in solo and spend some quality time catching up with Imp while Pa waits in the toasty car with Baby. Ma then goes out and gets Baby while Pa brings Imp out on a leash to replicate the test Baby introduction. Ma and Baby enter the house first and sit in a neutral room away the front door. Pa follows while telling leashed Imp how heavenly this fragrant little bundle is. Baby now gifts Imp with a treasure.

Heads up! *Until you know how Imp will respond to Baby's crying, if Baby's fussy on the ride home, best to wait for the crying to subside before the initial howdy-do.*

From here, maintain Imp's adjusted schedule while demonstrating that Baby is a quality of life enhancer. Ask guests to greet Imp before cooing over Baby—she won't mind. Then, have them hand Imp a goody that you've strategically placed for easy delivery. Social Imp will view company as a fringe benefit of Baby. Shy Imp may welcome being sent away to the den after saying hello. Ma's maternity leave is the best gift of all.

By day five, Imp should catch on that Baby's a keeper and between ten and fourteen days he'll be hard-pressed to remember life Baby-less.

Your next hurdle is when Baby becomes mobile. So far, the floor has been Imp's domain and the only crawling creatures he's encountered knew the meaning of a warning growl and enjoyed having their butts sniffed. Some dogs act as though they don't recognize this mobile being that they'd previously accepted as family.

In anticipation of Baby's mobility, desensitize Imp to the peculiar human activity by crawling around the floor yourself. His showing interest by wanting to sniff crawling you is perfectly natural and should be positively and calmly reinforced. Imp's trying to engage you in play with a tug toy or by pawing, though innocently intended, has to be discouraged. Tell him what a sweet boy he is and ask him to "go lie down" on the spot(s) you've rehearsed upfront. And if Imp is in the habit of denning beneath a table, desk or bed, to avoid a Precious-like response, discourage his doing so while redoubling his responsiveness to the Send

Away. Worse case, block Imp's access to these *de facto* dens. Just as he accepted Baby's presence, Imp should soon accept her mobility.

Of course there will be hurdles that will require fine-tuning. If Imp loves toys, don't overreact if he swipes Baby's. I have a hard time telling dog and kid toys apart, myself. And he'll be attracted to dirty diapers, so stash them securely away. Imp's a flexible guy and, as long as the key markers are met, life with Baby will soon be his new—and possibly improved—normal.

Red Flags!

The following Red Flags! are extremely rare and extremely serious. Should either develop, keep Baby and Imp apart and seek professional help immediately.

1. Baby's Squealing: Some dogs with high prey drive become overly aroused by Baby's shrieks and respond as they might to a wounded animal. Beware of Imp's extreme panting, whimpering, drooling, pointing, trembling and/or sustained fix-eyed staring.
2. The Onset Of Crawling: Occasionally, a dog becomes aroused and tries to nibble on the back of Baby's neck or to mount her.

CHAPTER 18

Introducing Imp to Incoming Impette

J ust as I don't believe in getting a dog for the kids, I don't believe in getting a second dog for the first. Get a second (or third, or fourth…) because you want to and hope that Imp agrees with your decision. Imp will probably be tickled, but I've met many first dogs who are indifferent to the second or seemed a bit resentful, so make sure this is still a commitment you are prepared to keep.

Ideally, wait until Imp is two to introduce Impette. By then, most of # 1's kinks should be ironed out and he's still young enough for fun. Because dogs of opposite sex are less apt to fight, if you only plan on having two, this is safest way to go. As I believe all companion Imps should be spayed or neutered, population control is a non-issue. More often than not, same-sex neutered dogs also get along great. Dogs of similar size play more equally, but I've known countless mismatched pairs who work it out. ReRun, my 105-pound shepherd-mix, was madly in love with a diminutive Pug named Michelle. Lying down, ReRun was the same height as Michelle standing so she'd run laps around his big old smiling, tail-wagging self.

In advance of Impette's arrival, give Imp a hint of what's imminent by readying the house as you had for him. Have an outfitted puppy crate set up near where Imp's crate had been or still is. Five days advance notice is plenty.

On the big homecoming day, remove #1's food bowl and choice toys or bones. Make sure #1 is well-exercised and, if #2 is also an adult, same deal. If there's a safe neutral place to introduce the two, that'd be easiest on #1.

Both dogs need their own handler who should speak happily about the other duo. Allow them to sniff one another on loosely held leashes for as long as it takes to relax. Now, take a tandem stroll before heading home. Have #1 enter the house or yard first and allow #2 to investigate his new digs while you supervise the two acting as though you haven't a care in the world. This might be a good time to break into song.

It helps to know #1's play style so you can quickly intervene if there's a deviation from it. The happier my DJ is the more grumbly and long-suffering he sounds in play. Uninitiated human ears find this disconcerting but other dogs recognize it as bluster.

From here, reassure #2 so he feels safe and secure while letting #1 know that he's still your main squeeze. Keep #1's pre-pup schedule as intact as possible. Added guests, walks, toys and treats will show #1 that #2 is a quality of life enhancer.

Be prepared for an altercation or two, especially in the beginning. Usually, they're just having "words," though a nip is not out of the question. Fifteen-year-old Kiana bit Cozy her first day here terrifying us both and making me feel horrible about endangering the 7-week-old sensitive puppy. From that day forth the two have been inseparable with Kiana babying Cozy, as she hadn't any of the others. I assume Kiana sensed that this exuberant bundle could soon overwhelm her and decided to pull the 'who's boss' bandage off fast. As with all relationships, there will probably be occasional disagreements. Unless either is in serious danger, it's best to walk away and let them work it out.

If you're worried that it's unfair to crate #2 if #1 is free—it's not. Would you worry about cribbing Baby when her older siblings sleep in bunk beds? And you don't need to do everything equally with each dog. As a matter of fact, it's important to separate them even if it's not actually necessary. There's nothing worse than poor Imp's being away from his pack for the first time when he's hospitalized with a broken leg.

Being single, I design one-on-one activities with each of my ten critters. Herbie Bird loves to cuddle under a blanket, Floozy accompanies me into the shower, DJ Dog enjoys running errands and Buddha never met a body of water she didn't dive into. Of course baby Cozy gets bonus time that I rationalize as being what each of her housemates had previously enjoyed. Dogs don't keep score.

In the beginning, be deferential to #1 by feeding him first and giving him dibs on proximity to his peeps. But please don't assume that #1's being there first means he is destined to be the top dog. This is typically difficult for dog parents to accept, as is the assumption that bigger is better. I just paid an "emergency" house call because the Miniature Poodle puppy has been bullying the five-year-old Standard whose peeps were appalled. As #1 seemed perfectly happy being second-in-command, I explained that projecting human values endangers the troops.

Dogs have their own hierarchies that need to unfold naturally, otherwise there's a good chance they'll fight. My Buddha, who is the second oldest, is the low dog by many rungs. Even meek baby Cozy has begun bossing Bu about. Though it breaks my heart to watch everyone pick on her, my having previously encouraged Buddha to assert herself got her in trouble with the higher-ups. Now, I simply walk away, dig out Bu's floaties and take her on a solo date to the lake.

CHAPTER 19

The Final Chapter
Elder Imp

Where Imp's infancy was intense by virtue of its brevity, every Elder I've lived with faded gracefully—up until the bitter end, that is. I'll defer to your veterinarian's recommendations nutrition and supplementation-wise. The following suggestions are designed to keep Elder safe while preserving his dignity.

It is common for old dogs to lose their hearing. This is typically a gradual process, worse on one side than the other. As you can imagine, it's disorienting for you both. Elder may no longer respond to his name or meet you at the door as before. He is apt to startle easily, occasionally snapping at whomever surprises him, much like some people lash out when awaked from a deep sleep. It's best to monitor toddlers and others whose movement or behavior is erratic.

Many deaf dogs respond to the vibration of a handclap, stomped foot or slammed door. If Elder still doesn't react, gently rock him reassuringly and stay close until he gets his bearings. Don't hover over him here.

To get Elder's attention after dark, flicker a flashlight or pointer that you previously paired with choice treats. Of course, make sure it's not aimed directly at his eyes. Same with flickering outdoor lights if Elder's in a fenced yard. Once he looks at you, kneel down, spread your arms and beckon Elder as you did when he was a pup.

Arthritic Elder may appreciate an orthopedic dog bed, and if he's large, a lift-assist harness. Keeping his routine as consistent as possible is especially important now. Go ahead and indulge sweet Elder with special snacks and bonus cuddle time. Why not?

The specifics of how to say goodbye are too personal and painful for me to presume what would be right for you. And there may be ethical implications that I dare not touch.

We all hope that Elder either peacefully slips away precisely when we're equipped to cope, or there will be a clear sign it's time to hasten the process. All too often, though, when this illusive harbinger is finally recognized, Imp's essence is already gone.

As an ardent proponent of death with dignity, this has guided me with my own Elders. All but once, that is. Thirty-eight years later, it still pains me to have allowed my beloved German Shepherd, Algunza, to suffer so

because of my misguided belief that there was a perfect way to say goodbye.

Since then, knowing that death was imminent and inevitable, I have held each of my Elders when euthanized, if possible, right here at home. And though I was profoundly sad, with sorrow the yin to acceptance's yang, there has also been a tender sweetness to the goodbye that made me proud to have participated. I pray that I, too, am ultimately afforded comparable compassion.

Mourning Imp

I don't believe we ever get "over" the loss of a loved one; we just get distance from the pain. Having said goodbye to too many dogs, I'd like to say it's gotten easier with experience. It has not. The only difference is that I now know I will survive.

Because Imp's life is so condensed, pleasure and pain are exaggerated. Perhaps dogs were selected as the most companionable creature on earth to teach us to make every moment matter. They do. Or maybe it's to settle the quality/quantity quandary once and for all.

Watching the utter glee with which Cozy just romped in the snow for thirty minutes will sustain me for hours. Would I want a watered-down dog if it meant prolonging her life? Possibly: but not today.

The intensity of grief varies from loss to loss, of course. I'd not sacrifice the depth of adoration of the most beloved in exchange for diminished heartache of losing the least. It pains me to hear of someone too traumatized to ever get another dog. The pleasure/pain ratio falls so in favor of new love. But that's me.

When I feel un-entitled to my emotions I go underground. Hide. That's why I'm writing, it's time to come out and hold my head high.

I have lost my husband, my parents and many more and know that mourning the death of a dog is as legitimate as mourning any other loss, and often more pure. Love is love. The heart has no hierarchy, it does not judge. Celebrate the love by honoring the loss. Imp would do so for you.

CHAPTER 20

Epilogue
In An ImPerfect World

I wrote most of this book five years ago and, for a number of reasons, stopped writing just like that. Much has changed. I've said goodbye to Kiana, DJ, Buddha and Bugsy Seagull. The dogs were 16, 14, and 15+. Bugsy's age was unknown. All but Kiana died within the past year. Updating the losses in real-time was too painful and distracting and not especially relevant, so I left the text as it was originally written. The parrot population is still six, though two of the players have changed.

I was diagnosed with Non-Hodgkin's Lymphoma in 2013. Having sailed through surgery, radiation and chemo, I'm doing great, thanks in large part to the critters. Déjà vu, Buddha and Bugsy were here through the worst of it. DJ Dog always knew the right thing to do.

A month into treatment, Herbie Bird unearthed a little something in my neck that ballooned into a colossal tumor. It was surgically removed soon thereafter. Cozy tried (hard) to minister to my post-surgical wounds. Later, her sounding the alarm in response to a scary drug reaction may well have saved my life. Sweet Cozy's been my rock throughout and the soft spot I can't wait to come home to.

I adopted Doc following DJ's passing. In the past, I waited what I believed to be a respectful mourning period before pursuing a new adoptee. This time, for reasons I couldn't immediately understand, I felt compelled to adopt fast. After asking my oncologist if he thought my adopting a puppy was crazy, with his emphatic, "Not crazy at all!" baby Doc arrived from Tennessee two weeks later. A grainy photo on Pet Finders was all I had to go on. This seeming impulsivity is something I'd have discouraged in others and judged in myself. That's when I accepted that the metrics of my life had been irreversibly redefined. Worry not; my first calls upon diagnosis were to make sure everyone would be well cared for when I go.

It's sunrise. Doc, who's been here nine months, is tunneled beneath the leopard-patterned throw, his head straddles Cozy's butt on their couch by the fire. Cozy spurs Doc's advances. He nails her tail that wags broadly below the blanket causing it, too, to wag. Apparently, this is even more entertaining than her naked tail had been. Someone passed gas. Speaking of which, you know how people blame their own toots on the dog? Historically, I've taken credit for theirs lest anyone thinks less of my mutts.

The parrots are beginning to rouse. Herbie's, "I love you, *mwaaah!*" is followed by an inside joke-like chuckle. Floozy's banging the breakfast bell while muttering emphatically in a tongue all her own. Now everyone's bell-banging. "I love you"s abound. Most of these birds and dogs and their predecessors were rescued from deplorable conditions too painful to ponder. That each now demonstrates such trust and resilience overwhelms my heart.

I have lived and worked with wildlife worldwide and companion animals here at home since the day I was born. Though my income is wanting, I get peed on regularly and just signaled, "stay'" to a hunky waiter who no doubt thinks I'm insane, a life devoted to cherishing animals and keeping them safe is beyond Good Enough for me.

The End.

ACKNOWLEDGMENTS

Bringing *Imp, the ImPerfect Pup* to life with Patty and Tina has unquestionably been a highlight of my life. Patty and I go back nearly thirty years. Tina and I: just a few. If two finer people exist anywhere, I'd sure love to meet them.

Patty and my friendship has been slow and steady—like a leisurely and loving stroll. Tina and mine: more of a spirited sprint. Tina and I met soon after my Lymphoma diagnosis. She and her gorgeous husband, Gerry, stepped up and took care of me in the gentlest, most respectful of ways. Gerry even proofread an early rendition of *Imp*. Patty, Tina, Gerry and I met through their dogs.

LAST BUT NOT LEAST, THANKS TO:

Boo Volpaccio, Konjo Swanke-Nichols, Rusty Dyslin, Flame Griffon, Hazel Hart, Milano Stiegler, Lakota Vaughan, Moses Keegan, Bentley Babcock, Zara Letezio, Enzo Bartovic, Fluffy Schwartz, Kibbles Parker, Blaze Oshin, Bella Gorab, Sno Foerster, Winnie Gordon, Wilson Dewan, Oona Shelley, Georgia McAvey, Benny Frank, Cecil Reilly, Mamie Vose, Willett Edwards, Sheba Buckley, Faith Russo, Twitch Haug, Bella Ambler, Red Ramsey, Bugsy Dresser, Ozzy Barrett, Kikuee Steinberg, Brio Miller,

Piper Tallman, Rupert Haney, Skippy Bialik, Ernie Lerner, Abbey Duvall, Charlie Epstein, Layla Gany, Sherlock Morton, Biscuit Thomsen, Emily Pfeffer, Trixie Kelly, Tucker Bluestein, Cloud Casey, Beau Kouzukian, Tigger Larobina, Tonto Tepper, Minnie Donaher, Sailor Coleman, Max Mariyappa, Addie Heyman, Bode Bassler, Kirby Suter, Isaac Ciardi, Brady Finnecy, Mojo Marino, Jake Costello, Oliver Mazza, Jaxon Albert, Nikki Taylor, Dusty Kelly, Percy Savage, Kiwi Hames, Stanley Brier, Candy Wattel, Happy Vicente, Buffet Alswanger, Ranger Pucci, Lux Mawat, Nate Brenner, Lupo Lieberman-Kaplan, Lilly Desmarteau, Murphy Wiseman, Odin Gonzales, Fudgie Farber, Oscar Champagne, Panti Fischer, Dylan Hannon, Fenway D'Amico, Bud Carpenter, Barney Struzzi, Lola Costa, Merle Atwater, Zoey Rosen, Tessa Gillies, Zoey Gough, Schatzi Krygier, Linus Konchalski, Bogey Hobson-Singleton, Timmy Schooler, Molly Lukens, Sally Cardo, Cooper Nadel, Angel Bogert, Thunder Lghtbourne, Bailey Bloch, Piper Rappoport, Toto Harbach, Indigo Schaefler, Charlie Fein, Sherlock Morton, Dexter Ackley, Lola McEnery, Oz Cramer, Chanel Roth, Deano Di Blasi, Mia Flynn, Juno Cohenuram, Zoe Yan, Peeve Blakely, Oakley Benedetto, Beau Soriano, Lucy Arbron, Brutus Chandler, Hans Solo Chapman, Kona Hilleman, Murphy Selter, Bunny Brody, Finnegan Shanley, Punch Tierney, Jackson Worthington, Sadie Abramson, Caine Wakeman, Ellie Daidone-Belardo, Zoey Rosen, Luigi Bruno, Gigi Biagi, Jesse Baker, Maia Beller, Luna Goff, Akira Mennitt, Lucky DiFiesta, Natalie Beitman, Phoebe Braverman, Chopper Kulbach, Oliver Parker, Emmy L'archesque, Lily Giff, Kona Gabel, Axel Eastman, Murray Storstrom, Parker Trinka, Gertie Calvert, Bentley Brown ....

Index

CPSIA information can be obtained
at www.ICGtesting.com
Printed in the USA
LVOW10s0231221116

514023LV00014B/235/P